I AM A WONDER WOMAN

PORTABLE
PRESS
San Diego, California

WRITTEN BY *Ellen Bailey*

ILLUSTRATED BY *Lauren Farnsworth*
and *Sophie Beer*

EDITED BY *Lauren Farnsworth*

DESIGNED BY *Kim Hankinson*

COVER DESIGN BY *Angie Allison*

CONSULTANCY BY *Emma Marriott*

This book is dedicated to Babs.

Portable Press
An imprint of Printers Row Publishing Group
10350 Barnes Canyon Road, Suite 100, San Diego, CA 92121
www.portablepress.com • e-mail: mail@portablepress.com

Publisher: Peter Norton
Associate Publisher: Ana Parker
Publishing/Editorial Team: April Farr, Vicki Jaeger, Tanya Fijalkowski, Lauren Taniguchi, Carrie Davis
Editorial Team: JoAnn Padgett, Melinda Allman, Dan Mansfield
Production Team: Jonathan Lopes, Rusty von Dyl

ISBN: 978-1-68412-548-7

Printed in China

22 21 20 19 18   1 2 3 4 5

Contents

Foreword

"IT'S TIME TO CELEBRATE. THERE HAS NEVER BEEN A MORE IMPORTANT TIME FOR GIRLS AND WOMEN TO FEEL *valued and empowered.*

The journey is not over yet, but we have come a long way, building on a history of incredible women who have paved the paths for success in every subject imaginable—from science, mathematics, and politics to art, design, and literature. Many of these women have been hidden behind the scenes or overlooked by their colleagues and historians. But now is the time for them to step into the light and get the recognition they deserve.

It is up to us to truly appreciate the sacrifices they have made, the adversities they have struggled through, and the achievements and contribution of their work. Achievements that make womankind an extraordinary family to belong to.

Remember, your accomplishments don't have to be groundbreaking or world famous for you to make a difference. We all have a light to shine and together we can be brighter than the sun. From the moment you get up in the morning,

you are a WONDER WOMAN. LET'S MAKE THE WORLD A BETTER PLACE FOR EVERYONE."

Dr. Maggie Aderin-Pocock, MBE, space scientist

How to use this book

This book was made just for you. Use this book to be inspired, to learn the histories of women across the globe, to discover facts and details you never knew before, and to step into the shoes of some of the most incredible women to have ever existed by getting involved in the activities.

There are thought-provoking questions, quizzes, make-and-do challenges, drawing projects, and much more to explore. But where to start? Take a look at the contents list and choose who you want to read about—it might be someone you're already familiar with or someone you have never heard of before.

At the end of the book there is space for you to design your very own entry. You can use these pages to think about why you are such an important person. Where have you come from? Where are you going? What do you want to achieve? No matter what your dreams are, you can take your place among these incredible figures.

ADA Lovelace

Ada was not only an awesome mathematician. She is also considered to be the world's first computer programmer.

Ada's dad was Lord Byron—he was quite a famous poet, but Ada's mom thought Lord Byron was a useless layabout. She wanted her daughter to be different. Ada was taught math and logic, and turned out to be a bit of a genius. She was even made to lie still for long periods of time to develop her self-control. Perhaps this is why she became interested in designing her own set of wings. At age 12 she investigated different materials and sizes for wings and wrote a book called *Flyology*.

THINGS TOOK OFF FOR ADA WHEN SHE WAS A TEENAGER AND MET MATHEMATICIAN CHARLES BABBAGE, WHO IS KNOWN AS "THE FATHER OF THE COMPUTER" BECAUSE HE INVENTED THE FIRST MECHANICAL COMPUTER. BUT IT WAS ADA WHO EXPLAINED BEFORE ANYONE ELSE THAT COMPUTERS COULD BE USED TO CARRY OUT A SET OF INSTRUCTIONS, KNOWN AS AN ALGORITHM.

British mathematician
1815 – 1852

Sadly Ada died young, at 36 years old, but not before she had made her mark as one of the most important names in computing history.

What's an ALGORITHM?

Algorithms are incredibly important to modern computing, and are essential to the way computers process information, or data. Using algorithms, computers can carry out useful tasks, such as calculating complicated sums or printing large amounts of material.

The CHEESE sandwich CHALLENGE

Computer coding is all about breaking big tasks down into small steps. Put yourself to the test and see if you can write an algorithm for making a cheese sandwich.

1. Buy CHEESE AND BREAD
Write down detailed step-by-step instructions for making a cheese sandwich. Make sure that you include every single detail and that all the steps are in the correct order.

2. Test THE CODE
Give your code (and all the ingredients and materials needed) to a friend. Ask them to follow the instructions as if they're a robot who has never made a sandwich before. They are not allowed to do anything that isn't written down.

3. DEBUG
Has your friend made a normal-looking sandwich? If yes, congratulations, your algorithm worked. If no, debug your code by adding in additional steps or switching them around.

4. Test and DEBUG
Repeat the test until your code is flawless and the sandwich is delicious!

Amelia EARHART

1897 – 1937

AMERICAN AVIATION PIONEER AND AUTHOR

"Women must try to do things as men have tried. When they fail, their failure must be but a challenge to others."

WHY WAS AMELIA AWESOME?

- In 1932, she set out to become the first female pilot to fly solo across the Atlantic Ocean.

- She took off from Newfoundland. To keep up her strength she sipped tomato juice through a straw.

- Just under 15 hours later she landed safely in Ireland in a field full of startled cows. She had set a new Atlantic flight record.

- She wrote bestselling books about her experiences and helped form The Ninety-Nines, an organization for female pilots.

- Amelia set out to fly around the world in 1937, but disappeared in the mid-Pacific and was never seen again.

WHY WOULD BEING A PILOT BE AMAZING?

- -

- -

- -

- -

IF YOU COULD FLY TO ANYWHERE IN THE WORLD, WHERE WOULD YOU GO?

- -

- -

- -

- -

WHAT WOULD YOU EAT ON YOUR FLIGHT TO STAY STRONG?

- - - - - - - - - - - - - - - - - - -

- - - - - - - - - - - - - - - - - - -

- - - - - - - - - - - - - - - - - - -

DRAW A MAP OF THE PLACES YOU'VE FLOWN TO.

Amelia's Vega Monoplane

AMNA
Al Haddad

Professional weightlifter from the United Arab Emirates

STARTED WEIGHTLIFTING AT 19 YEARS OLD

Former journalist who wrote about inspirational young women

Uses her success to make weightlifting accessible to other women

First and only Muslim woman to compete in the Asia Regional CrossFit Games in a headscarf in 2012

With Nike, she designed their Pro Hijab—a breathable, lightweight head covering that can be worn by Muslim athletes

IS AN INSPIRATIONAL SPEAKER AND ENCOURAGES GIRLS TO PURSUE SPORTS PROFESSIONALLY

Want to try it?

Fill out the tick-box list below. You might be like Amna and find you develop a passion for something you'd never considered before. Make it your mission to try as many of these sports over the coming year as you can.

Sport	Would like to try it	Tried it	Loved it!
Archery			
Badminton			
Basketball			
Boxing			
Cycling			
Diving			
Fencing			
Football			
Golf			
Gymnastics			
Handball			
Hockey			
Judo			
Rowing			
Sailing			
Soccer			
Softball			
Swimming			
Table Tennis			
Taekwondo			
Tennis			
Track and Field			
Trampoline			
Volleyball			
Water polo			
Weightlifting			
Wrestling			

Anandibai JOSHI

Indian doctor

1865 - 1887

At the time that Anandibai was born in India there were no female doctors in the country. Very few girls even went to school. Anandibai was married at the extremely young age of 9 to a man called Gopalrao Joshi.

Gopalrao wanted to help Anandibai get an education. One day, when he found Anandibai helping her grandmother to cook, he said she should get back to her books! This was a very unusual attitude in India at that time.

When Anandibai was 14 she had a baby boy, but he only lived for ten days. Anandibai wanted to help prevent other people from suffering this kind of tragedy. She addressed the people who lived in Serampore and told them that she wanted to go to America to train as a doctor. She explained that there was a need for female doctors and that she wanted to open a medical college for women in India. Her message spread across the country and lots of people supported her and gave her money.

Anandibai fulfilled her dream and graduated from the Women's Medical College of Pennsylvania at the age of 20 and returned to India to a triumphant welcome. She died the following year from tuberculosis and was mourned across the country, but she had paved the way for a new generation of female doctors in India.

Women's WORK

JOB	What woman or girl do you know who would be awesome at this job?

When I grow up I want to be a

I would be amazing at this because ...

13

Age 8

Anna sees a ballet performance of *The Sleeping Beauty* and instantly knows what she wants to do with her life.

Age 10

Anna enrolls at the Imperial Ballet School. Ballerinas at this time tend to be small and compact, but Anna has long limbs. The other students make fun of Anna because of her body shape.

Age 18

Anna's teachers can see she is talented and works hard. Anna graduates as a "coryphée," which means she can skip the stage in her career where ballerinas have to dance in large groups.

Anna PAVLOVA

Russian ballerina

1881 - 1931

Age 24

Anna dances the lead solo in *The Dying Swan*. Her masterful technique, swan-like limbs, and expressive movements tell the story perfectly. The audience is captivated.

Age 30

Anna sets up her own dance company. It is one of the first to tour ballet around the world. She brings ballet to new audiences who have never seen this kind of dancing before. She inspires children from all different countries to become ballerinas, just as she'd been inspired all those years ago.

Even Anna's feet were "apparently" all wrong; they were rigid and had high arches. Anna fixed the problem by adding extra support to her ballet shoes, and so the modern pointe shoe was born!

Dear me ...

Imagine how it must have felt for Anna when the other student dancers laughed at her because of what she looked like. Think of a time when you have experienced something similar, or even just worried about what other people were thinking. Write a letter addressed to yourself to let you know why you should not let things like this stop you achieving your dreams—just like Anna!

Anna's ballet shoes from 1920

Anne
FRANK

GERMAN DIARIST
1929 – 1945

Anne Frank is the author of one of the most famous books in the world—her diary.

Anne was born in Germany, but when she was four her family moved to the Netherlands, as the Nazi Party gained control of Germany. The Nazi Party persecuted many groups of people, in particular people of Jewish heritage, which Anne and her family were.

During World War II, the Nazis occupied the Netherlands and the Frank family were in such danger that they went into hiding from 1942. They lived in a secret annex that was concealed behind a movable bookshelf at her father's workplace. The annex was a few rooms shared by the Franks and four other people. The employees at the workplace took care of everyone in hiding, bringing them supplies. It was a task that became more difficult with each passing day.

Anne received her diary for her 13th birthday, just before she went into hiding. She dreamed of being a journalist or a famous author. Her diary describes her life, from the difficulties of living in such a confined space to the relationships between her family members. It is a touching account of what it's like to be a teenage girl.

Sadly, after two years in hiding, the family were arrested by Nazi police and sent to concentration camps. Anne died of typhus a few months later at the age of 15, but her diary lives on—it has sold over 30 million copies and has been translated into 67 languages.
It teaches the world about the dangers of prejudice and discrimination.

MY DIARY

Write your own diary entry here. What might people in the future be interested in hearing about from your life? What are your feelings about the people you live with? Do you have any hopes and dreams for the future?

ANNIE *Londonderry*

LATVIAN-AMERICAN CYCLIST

1870 – 1947

Annie takes on the world ... literally

IN 1894, IT WAS CLAIMED THAT TWO RICH BOSTON MEN PLACED A BET THAT NO WOMAN COULD TRAVEL AROUND THE WORLD BY BICYCLE IN 15 MONTHS. ENTER ANNIE COHEN KOPCHOVSKY, A MARRIED MOTHER OF THREE CHILDREN, WHO TOOK ON THE CHALLENGE, HAVING NEVER EVEN RIDDEN A BICYCLE UNTIL A FEW DAYS BEFORE HER TRIP.

Money maker

Annie was a brilliant saleswoman and her first sponsor was the Londonderry Lithia Spring Water Company of New Hampshire. They paid her $100 to use the name "Annie Londonderry" throughout the trip. She attached posters and banners advertising lots of different companies to her bicycle, to make money as she cycled the world.

Off and away

Annie set off on her journey wearing a long skirt and corset, but was so uncomfortable she soon switched to wearing a man's riding suit. She became a global celebrity as she toured Chicago, New York, Paris, Marseilles, Alexandria, Colombo, Singapore, Saigon, Hong Kong, Shanghai, and San Francisco on her bike. She was a skillful publicist and was forever in the newspapers, challenging people's perceptions of what Victorian women should, and could, do. She faced a mountain of hardships on her way, but returned victorious to collect her prize money of $10,000—with 14 days to spare!

WHAT PERILS DID ANNIE OVERCOME?

- SHE LOST A LARGE AMOUNT OF WEIGHT.
- SHE FACED TERRIBLE WEATHER CONDITIONS.
- HER BIKE AND MONEY WERE CONFISCATED IN FRANCE.
- SHE INJURED HER FOOT ON THE ROAD.
- SHE WAS ALMOST KILLED BY A RUNAWAY HORSE AND WAGON.
- SHE BROKE HER WRIST CRASHING INTO A GROUP OF PIGS.

BIKE TO
brilliance

READ THE QUESTIONS BELOW AND JOT DOWN YOUR THOUGHTS. THEY MAY INSPIRE YOU TO UNDERTAKE AN AMAZING JOURNEY ONE DAY.

If you were going to cycle around the world, what place would you be most excited to visit?

If you could only take three possessions with you, what would they be?

If you were away from home for 15 months, what would you miss the most?

Which one of Annie's perils sounds the worst to have encountered?

Annie's Sterling bicycle, on which she completed the majority of her trip

Artemisia GENTILESCHI

Italian painter

1593 – circa 1652

Artemisia's mother died when she was just 12 years old. Her father, Orazio Gentileschi, was a painter and, instead of sending his daughter to school, he took her to his studio to teach her to be an artist. He taught her how to draw, how to mix colors, and how to paint.

Orazio was inspired by the artist Caravaggio, whose dramatic style of contrasting light and shadow can be seen in Artemisia's work. At the age of 17, Artemisia produced an incredible artwork called *Susanna and the Elders*. The Italian art world could see she was wildly talented, and she became the first woman to be accepted into the Accademia delle Arti del Disegno (Academy of the Arts of Drawing).

Artemisia loved to paint pictures of strong, courageous, and powerful women. Many of her paintings show women from the Bible and myths, but tell their stories from the women's perspective. They encourage the viewer to think about these stories in new ways. Artemisia's paintings have great expressive strength and demonstrate her supreme technical ability. She is one of the greatest painters of her time.

Draw a tribute

CAN YOU THINK OF A GIRL OR WOMAN IN YOUR LIFE WHO YOU REALLY ADMIRE? IT COULD BE YOUR MOM, YOUR SISTER, OR EVEN A FRIEND. DRAW A PORTRAIT OF THEM BELOW, SHOWING HOW STRONG AND WONDERFUL YOU THINK THEY ARE.

Brita TOTT

Danish spy & forger

DATES OF BIRTH AND DEATH UNKNOWN, BUT LIVING CIRCA 1498

Danish-born, 15th-century noblewoman Brita Tott became one of the world's most effective spies. She got married and moved to Sweden. There she became great friends with King Charles of Sweden. But when Sweden and Denmark went to war, she still felt very loyal to her homeland.

She used the King to get the gossip on Sweden's battle plans. Then she betrayed the King and told her pals back in Denmark everything. She was caught and sentenced to burn at the stake, but managed to persuade them to let her just stay imprisoned in a nunnery for a while. She also forged documents to increase her fortune and created fake wax seals. Brita wasn't going to let anyone push her around.

Can you forge Brita's signature?

COULD YOU BE A SPY?

ANSWER THE QUESTIONS BELOW, RATING YOURSELF ON EACH SCALE FROM 1 - 5.

1. How important is it to you to be able to talk about what you've done at school with your friends and family?

Very important   Unimportant

1   2   3   4   5

2. Do you like to follow a set routine or are you happy to do things at different times each day?

Set routine   Different each day

1   2   3   4   5

3. Do you prefer to always work with your friends or do you like to meet and work with new people?

Work with friends   Work with new people

1   2   3   4   5

4. Do you like to figure problems out by yourself or to work collaboratively as part of a team?

Alone   Collaboratively

1   2   3   4   5

5. How good are you at keeping secrets?

Hopeless—I always end up telling!   Excellent—I never tell!

1   2   3   4   5

ADD UP YOUR SCORE. THE CLOSER IT IS TO 25, THE MORE SUITABLE YOU ARE FOR A CAREER IN ESPIONAGE.

THE BRONTË SISTERS

1816 – 1855

Charlotte

1818 – 1848

Emily

1820 – 1849

Anne

British authors

Charlotte, Emily, and Anne grew up in a little village called Haworth in England. Their house backed on to the Yorkshire moors—a wild, isolated place that sparked the children's imaginations. With no televisions or computers back then, they had to come up with other ways of having fun.

One day, their father gave them a set of 12 wooden soldiers. They absolutely loved them and invented a fictional world called "Glass Town" for the soldiers to live in. They made tiny books for the soldiers and filled them with poems, stories, drawings, and maps.

The girls' passion for writing developed, and in 1846 they published a book of poems they had written. They worried that the world might not be interested in the writing of three unknown girls, so they published it under the pseudonyms Currer (Charlotte), Ellis (Emily), and Acton (Anne) Bell.

Beautiful Brontë novels

THE SISTERS' NOVELS WERE LATER PUBLISHED AND ARE LOVED AND ADMIRED TO THIS DAY.

CHARLOTTE

The oldest of the children, clever and ambitious. Authored *Jane Eyre*, *Shirley*, *Villette* and *The Professor*.

EMILY

Very shy and was only ever happy at home. Her one published novel, *Wuthering Heights*, changed the course of English literature.

ANNE

A girl who appeared mild but was fiercely passionate about women's rights. Authored *Agnes Grey* and *The Tenant of Wildfell Hall*.

Build a book

The Brontë sisters prove that you don't have to have epic life experiences to be a great writer. Follow in the Brontës' footsteps and make your own miniature book by following the instructions below. Fill it with poems or a short story.

1.
Take an 8.5 x 11 piece of paper and fold it in half lengthwise so that the two long sides meet.

2.
Now fold it in half again so that the two short sides meet.

3.
Then fold it in half again.

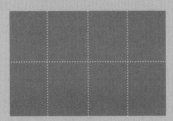

4.
Now unfold the piece of paper so that you have a sheet with 8 rectangles on it.

STOP CUTTING HERE!

5.
Fold the paper in half again so that the two short sides meet, then cut from the fold to the cross in the center.

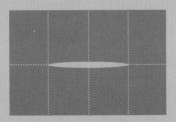

6.
Unfold the piece of paper. It should now have a slit along the middle. Fold it in half so that the two long edges meet.

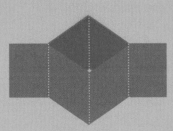

7.
Push the folded edges toward the center. The slit should open up into a diamond shape.

8.
Keep pushing until the folded edges meet in the middle, then fold the pages all together to make a book.

9.
You're finished. Now you just need to fill it with genius ideas!

Catherine
THE GREAT

Russian empress

1729 – 1796

Who was Catherine?

Catherine was Empress of Russia for over 30 years and was one of the country's most influential rulers. She was the daughter of a German royal family and was born in Prussia (now Szczecin in Poland). At the age of 16 she married Grand Duke Peter, who was the heir to the Russian throne.

WHAT ABOUT THIS PETER FELLOW?

Peter was horrible and was terrible at being the Emperor. The people of Russia didn't like him, but they loved Catherine. In fact, someone disliked Peter so much that they assassinated him and Catherine became Empress.

WHAT MADE CATHERINE "GREAT"?

Catherine had all sorts of great ideas about how she could make life better for the people of Russia. She was into education and culture. She thought that people should be given the opportunity to learn about art, music, literature, and science. She wanted to free the "serfs," peasants who where bound to a property and did all the hard farming work for the country.

So what happened then?

Of course, the people who owned the serfs didn't like the idea of freeing them. Catherine was forced to abandon her big ideas and focus on making Russia powerful. She did a really good job of it, and at the end of her reign Russia had expanded westward and southward over an area of more than 200,000 square miles. The era of her reign is known as the Golden Age of the Russian Empire.

Free the serfs!

While serfs were not technically slaves, they were not free either.

Serfs belonged to a property and were required to work for the master who owned the property, whether they liked it or not. Imagine you are Catherine and write a letter trying to convince a wealthy property owner to free their serfs.

CLEOPATRA

Ancient Egyptian pharaoh

CIRCA 69 BCE — 30 BCE

Cleopatra co-ruled ancient Egypt for almost three decades. She could speak at least nine languages and was educated in mathematics, philosophy, oratory, and astronomy. Everyone who met her was impressed. At the time of her rule, the Roman Empire was expanding and Egypt was at risk of losing its power, but Cleopatra used her skills as a negotiator to make links with influential people who would help keep her on the throne.

She was clearly a shrewd woman. When Roman Emperor Julius Caesar was in town to settle a dispute between her and her brother, Cleopatra devised a plan to make sure she met him first. She wrapped herself in a carpet and was smuggled into his private quarters. Caesar was so impressed with the Queen that he had her reinstalled with military support. Cleopatra and Caesar became allies. But when Caesar was killed, Cleopatra sided with a Roman politician and general named Mark Antony against Caesar's legal heir. She went to meet Antony dressed as a goddess, and arrived on a lavish purple boat with golden sails. Antony, who liked to think of himself as a bit of a god, thought this was brilliant. The two fell in love.

Antony and Cleopatra combined their armies and went into battle against Antony's enemies. But they lost and Antony, thinking that Cleopatra was dead, took his own life. Historians disagree on how Cleopatra met her end—some say she allowed herself to be bitten by a deadly Egyptian cobra and others say she drank a cup of poison.

Set the SCENE

The story of Cleopatra's life has been told by many filmmakers and playwrights, including William Shakespeare. Choose the episode from Cleopatra's life you find most inspiring and write a short scene for a play about how you think the event played out.

Cleopatra's name in hieroglyphs!

CORA Coralina

Brazilian poet

1889 ~ 1985

Cora Coralina, which means "red heart," was chosen as a pseudonym by a poet called Ana Lins dos Guimarães Peixoto Bretas. As a child Ana had a hobby that everyone around her thought was very strange: she loved reading. But Ana didn't care if people thought she was odd; she wanted to be a poet.

Ana led a busy life that didn't leave much time to become a published poet. She raised six children and worked in a bakery. But no matter where her life took her, she held on to her dream. When she was 70 Ana decided it was time to get serious with her poetry. She took a typing course so that she could send her poems off to publishers. She was the oldest person in the school, and became a symbol of courage and persistence for the younger students.

In 1965, her first book was finally published and she became one of Brazil's most important writers. She was described as being more powerful and influential than the rich rulers of the state. Her poetry has been compared to running water—clear, powerful, and natural. Her poems allow the reader to dive deep into life in the state of Goiás, where she was born and raised.

Todas as Vidas (ALL LIVES)

Ana's poem "All Lives" talks about the different identities that she has, and she describes each of these identities as a person that lives inside her: she is a washerwoman who washes clothes on the banks of the river; she is a cook who makes the dinner; she is a superstitious peasant who believes in magic; she is a mother with lots of children.

Do you feel like you have more than one identity? Maybe living inside you there is a daughter, a friend, a scientist, and an athlete. List the different identities that live inside you.

Inside me lives ...

Inside me lives ...

Inside me lives ...

Inside me lives ...

Elizabeth I

Queen of England

1533 - 1603

WHEN ARE YOU GOING TO GET MARRIED, LIZ?

"I will have but one mistress here, AND NO MASTER!"

Age 2
Elizabeth's mother, Anne Boleyn, the disgraced second wife of Henry VIII, is beheaded. Life's not off to a good start for the young princess.

Age 20
Henry VIII is dead. Elizabeth's half-sister, Mary, is now Queen. She accuses Elizabeth of treason and locks her up in the Tower of London. Not good— but Elizabeth has enough supporters in government to convince Mary to spare her.

Age 25
Elizabeth becomes Queen when Mary dies. Mary was not very popular so the country rejoices in their new Queen.

Age 33
The government refuses to give Elizabeth any more money unless she gets married. She tells them to get lost. Although deeply shocking at first, this decision became the cornerstone of her success. She was to stamp her authority on her court and government.

Age 50
Her reign as Queen is known as the Golden Age. Theater flourishes in England so Shakespeare is busy, and many English explorers sail to new lands.

Age 54
Under Elizabeth's command British troops defeat the Spanish Armada—a fleet of Spanish ships that set sail hoping to invade England and remove Elizabeth from the throne. The world gets the message—don't mess with Queen Liz.

Age 69
Elizabeth dies a beloved Queen, famous for ruling over one of the most exciting times in English history.

POSTCARD FROM THE TOWER OF LONDON

- - - - - - - - - - - - - - - - - -

- - - - - - - - - - - - - - - - - -

- - - - - - - - - - - - - - - - - -

- - - - - - - - - - - - - - - - - -

- - - - - - - - - - - - - - - - - -

- - - - - - - - - - - - - - - - - -

- - - - - - - - - - - - - - - - - -

- - - - - - - - - - - - - - - - - -

Imagine you had a sister who locked you up in the Tower of London because she thought you'd done something wrong. What a betrayal!

Send a postcard to her telling her how you feel. Why not design your stamp?

SPEAK UP

Elizabeth had a fiery temper. What do you think she said to the court when they tried to bully her into getting married? Write a speech for Elizabeth to give about not being pressured into doing something.

Ellie SIMMONDS

BRITISH PARALYMPIAN

Born 1994

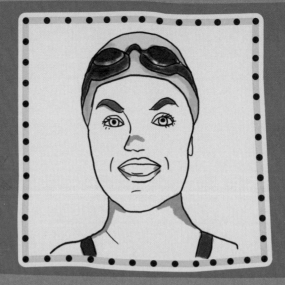

Ellie is a champion swimmer who was born in England. She has a disability called achondroplasia (a type of dwarfism), which means that her arms and legs are short compared to the rest of her body.

What's so excellent about Ellie?

She started swimming competitively against able-bodied children at the age of 8.

She made a huge splash when she won her first Paralympic medal at the age of 13.

Ellie has always believed in herself and knows she can do anything anybody else can do.

Her philosophy is that there's no point in being sad or hating who you are—you have to embrace life.

At the London 2012 Paralympics she won four medals: two golds, a silver, and a bronze.

She has numerous world records to her name.

At 14, she became the youngest person ever to receive an MBE (Member of the Order of the British Empire) from Queen Elizabeth II.

She balanced the demands of training with school work and public appearances.

Ellie is an ambassador for WaterAid and patron of the Dwarf Sports Association, a charity that helps people of restricted growth get into sports.

Love YOUR LIFE

ELLIE'S BIG SMILE AND POSITIVE ATTITUDE SHINE THROUGH IN EVERYTHING SHE DOES. SHE LOVES THE AMAZING THINGS HER BODY CAN DO. WRITE DOWN TEN AMAZING THINGS THAT YOUR BODY CAN DO.

NUMBER 1

1. ....

2. ....

3. ....

4. ....

5. ....

6. ....

7. ....

8. ....

9. ....

10. ....

If Ellie met you she'd tell you that you can do anything you want to do.
Why not set yourself a physical challenge, then go out there and smash it?

Elvira was born in Peru, but when World War II broke out she was living the high life in England.

Elvira CHAUDOIR

PERUVIAN DOUBLE AGENT

1913 – circa 1996

ELVIRA'S FRIENDS THOUGHT SHE WAS:

NOT INTERESTED IN POLITICS

Mostly interested in playing poker

A girl who liked a good party

THE GERMAN MILITARY THOUGHT SHE WAS:

Loyally working as a spy for them

SENDING TOP-SECRET INTELLIGENCE FROM BRITAIN

BUT ACTUALLY SHE WAS:

A BRITISH DOUBLE AGENT SENDING FALSE INTELLIGENCE TO THE GERMAN MILITARY

Instrumental in defeating the Nazis in World War II

WORKING FOR THE BRITISH GOVERNMENT UNDER THE CODENAME "BRONX"

Sending fake coded messages that sent Nazi troops in the wrong direction

SECRET *letters*

Elvira was taught how to use invisible ink by the British government, using a matchstick that had been dipped into a chemical powder. She wrote letters that seemed to contain nothing more than gossip about her social life, but in between the lines she wrote her intelligence reports in invisible ink that could be revealed using another chemical.

WRITE YOUR OWN SECRET MESSAGE

Here's how to make your own invisible ink to share secrets with your friends.

1.
MIX TOGETHER EQUAL AMOUNTS OF BAKING SODA AND WATER.

2.
DIP A COTTON SWAB IN THE MIXTURE AND WRITE YOUR MESSAGE ON A SHEET OF PAPER.

3.
TELL YOUR FRIEND TO USE A BRUSH TO PAINT GRAPE JUICE ACROSS THE PAGE. YOUR SECRET MESSAGE WILL REVEAL ITSELF!

Emmeline PANKHURST
BRITISH SUFFRAGETTE 1858 – 1928

When Emmeline was born in England, men were allowed to vote but women weren't. She was not happy about that at all. Both Emmeline's parents had a strong interest in politics, and she was only 14 when she was first introduced to the women's suffrage movement, which fought for women's right to vote. When Emmeline was older, she founded a group called the Women's Social and Political Union (WSPU). They believed in "deeds not words" and did all sorts of things to gain attention.

Emmeline's to-do list:

- Make a speech about women's rights
  - GET AS MANY PEOPLE AS POSSIBLE TO SIGN A PETITION
- Organize a rally
  - PUBLISH THIS WEEK'S *VOTES FOR WOMEN* NEWSPAPER
- Smash shop windows
  - SET FIRE TO A STATELY HOME

Chaining oneself to railings isn't the best way to get a point across, but Emmeline believed desperate measures were needed. She was repeatedly arrested and jailed three times, but didn't see herself as a law breaker. She saw herself as someone who was trying to become a law maker. In 1918 the law was changed so that women over the age of 30 who were property owners were allowed to vote. This was great news but still unfair because men were allowed to vote from the age of 21. Emmeline continued to fight for women's rights up until her death on June 14, 1928. Just a few weeks later all women over 21 years were allowed to vote. Go, sister suffragettes!

VOTES FOR WOMEN

In 1907, Emmeline's WSPU started up the newspaper *Votes for Women*, which became well known for its in-depth articles. Write an article for the front page about why you think women should be able to vote, just the same as men.

Emmy NOETHER

GERMAN MATHEMATICIAN

1882 – 1935

Emmy's dad was a mathematician, but as a child she learned the arts expected of a middle-class girl. As she grew older she set out to become a language teacher, but realized while she was at university that, actually, she was really, really good at math. In fact, she became one of the most important mathematicians in history. She devised a collection of beautiful theorems that changed long-held understandings in algebra and physics. Even Albert Einstein was seriously impressed. Everyone knew how brilliant Emmy was, but because at that time women weren't officially allowed to work in universities, she worked for no pay for over ten years. Can you imagine that? For a while she carried out her research and taught under a man's name, but, eventually, she was allowed to join the team officially.

Trouble struck when the Nazi Party came into power in Germany and, as someone of Jewish heritage, Emmy was again prevented from working in a university. Instead she moved to the United States and continued her work at Bryn Mawr College in Pennsylvania. One of Emmy's theorems, which is known as Noether's first theorem, has been described as one of the most important theorems ever proved in guiding the development of modern physics.

WHAT IS A THEOREM?

A theorem is a proven mathematical or scientific statement. An example is Pythagoras' theorem, which states that for any right-angled triangle, the square of the hypotenuse (the side opposite the right angle) is equal to the sum of the squares of the other two sides.

Looking AHEAD

Are you set on what you want to do in life, just like Emmy was before she discovered her talent in math? Write a list of every career you think you might enjoy and think of ways you could try them all out.

Career	How can I explore it?
Veterinary nurse	Volunteer at an animal shelter or take on responsibility for a pet

THINK THROUGH a theorem

Can you prove that no more than four colors are needed to color in this pattern so that no two adjacent regions have the same color? The only thing you need to do to prove this theorem is color it in!

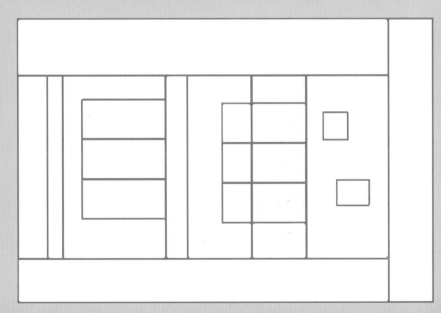

Eufrosina CRUZ

MEXICAN ACTIVIST

Born 1979

Eufrosina was born in a small town in Oaxaca, Mexico.

BEFORE EUFROSINA, IN THIS TOWN ...

... GIRLS OFTEN LEFT SCHOOL EARLY TO GET MARRIED AND HAVE BABIES.

... MEN WERE IN CHARGE.

... WOMEN COULD NOT VOTE WITHOUT THEIR HUSBANDS OR MALE FAMILY MEMBER PRESENT.

Then Eufrosina came along

Eufrosina wanted something different. When she was 11 she left the town to study in a city, and returned a few years later an educated young woman. She decided to run for mayor. The men of the town laughed at her. They said no one would vote for her, but many, many people did. Even though Eufrosina won the vote, the men still would not allow her to be in charge.

... Eufrosina fought to change things. She set up an association called QUIEGO, to help women fight for their rights. Thanks to Eufrosina, the law in Mexico was changed so that women could vote unaccompanied and could be in charge. Eufrosina became the mayor of her town. People kept voting her into more and more powerful positions, until she was in charge of the organization that makes laws for the whole of Oaxaca.

TODAY IN THE STATE OF OAXACA ...

... BOTH MEN AND WOMEN CAN BE IN CHARGE.

... WOMEN CAN VOTE UNACCOMPANIED AND HOWEVER THEY LIKE.

... GIRLS CAN FOLLOW IN EUFROSINA'S FOOTSTEPS AND CHOOSE WHAT THEY WANT TO DO WITH THEIR LIVES.

Flower power

Eufrosina chose the white lily as the symbol of her fight for the rights of native women. In Oaxaca, these flowers grow wild all over the countryside. They are resistant and strong, but also fragile.

Choose a flower that you think represents you. For example, you might choose a sunflower if you are always joyful and sunny. Turn your flower into a symbol and draw it in the space below.

Can you think of five words that describe both the flower and you?

Fadumo DAYIB

BORN 1972

SOMALI ACTIVIST

Fadumo was nicknamed Deeqo, which means "the sufficient," because she was the first of her mother's children to live to adulthood. Eleven of her siblings had died from treatable medical conditions before Fadumo was born.

Despite living in poverty, Fadumo's parents were determined to give their daughter an education. But Fadumo's schooling ended when her family was deported from Kenya to Somalia. Soon after, civil war erupted in Somalia and Fadumo ended up in Finland as a refugee.

In Finland, Fadumo found freedom: the freedom to study and the freedom to dream. She dreamed of returning to Somalia and improving the lives of the people who live there, especially the women and children. She went to college to learn about health, education, and the way that governments work.

Fadumo didn't start to learn to read until she was 11, but ended up as a Harvard graduate—impressive!

In 2014, Fadumo decided to run as Somalia's first female candidate for president. This was a brave move because many people didn't want to see change in the country. Fadumo received death threats, but she took them as a compliment—it meant people were taking her seriously. But in 2016 she decided to pull out because she believed that the election was corrupt and unethical. She said that she couldn't go against her values. Despite this, she has declared that she intends to be involved in making Somalia a better place for its citizens.

BEING A REFUGEE

BECOMING A REFUGEE MAY SEEM LIKE A STRANGE THING TO YOU, BUT IT HAPPENS TO PEOPLE ALL OVER THE WORLD. WHEN FADUMO LEFT SOMALIA FOR FINLAND, SHE PACKED A SUITCASE WITH PHOTOS OF HER PARENTS AND SMALL TREASURES FROM HOME. IF YOU WERE FORCED TO FLEE YOUR COUNTRY, WHICH 5 THINGS WOULD YOU TAKE WITH YOU?

1. ....

2. ....

3. ....

4. ....

5. ....

RUN FOR PRESIDENT!

When candidates run for president of their country, they come up with policies and promises that they intend to deliver to the people. Imagine you are running for president. What three promises would you make to the people of your country?

1. ....

2. ....

3. ....

She could easily have become a very rich lady of leisure, but wanted to help people instead.

BRITISH FOUNDER OF MODERN NURSING

THE FLORENCE NIGHTINGALE MEDAL is the highest international achievement a nurse can earn.

Cared for wounded soldiers in the Crimean War

Florence NIGHTINGALE

THE NIGHTINGALE PLEDGE is taken by new nurses to this day.

Her published works focused on spreading medical knowledge.

1820 – 1910

Became known as The Lady with the Lamp

Her SOCIAL REFORMS improved health care for British society and hunger relief in India.

INTERNATIONAL NURSES DAY is celebrated around the world on her birthday.

Back to BASICS

Florence was a big fan of basic hygiene standards that made hospitals cleaner and safer places. She showed that clean hospitals helped sick and injured people get better. Below are some personal hygiene tips that everyone is encouraged to follow to help eliminate the germs that can make us unwell. Fill in what to do and when to do it. The first one has been completed for you.

HAND HYGIENE

WHAT TO DO:
Thoroughly wash hands with warm water and soap.

WHEN TO DO IT:
Before and after eating, after playing with animals, after playing outside, after using the toilet.

CHANGING CLOTHES

WHAT TO DO:
....
....
....

WHEN TO DO IT:
....
....
....

MOUTH AND TEETH HYGIENE

WHAT TO DO:
....
....
....

WHEN TO DO IT:
....
....

BATHS AND SHOWERS

WHAT TO DO:
....
....

WHEN TO DO IT:
....
....
....

FRIDA KAHLO

Mexican painter

1907 – 1954

What was Frida's childhood like?

When Frida was six she caught an illness called polio and had to stay in bed for nine months. And even when she was better she wasn't completely better. Her right foot and leg were damaged by the disease and she walked with a limp.

What were Frida's dreams?

She wanted to become a doctor, and when she was 15 she enrolled in the elite National Preparatory School to study science. The school had only just started admitting girls. Of 2,000 students at the school, only 35 of them were girls.

What happened to Frida?

When Frida was 18, she was on a bus that crashed into a streetcar. A steel handrail went through Frida's hip and came out the other side. She fractured her legs and collarbone, and damaged her back. She was forced to stay in bed again, and had to wear an uncomfortable plaster corset.

How did she discover painting?

Frida had the idea that maybe she could become a medical artist. Her mother set up a special easel so that she could paint while lying in bed. Frida began to paint self-portraits and pictures of her friends. The pictures are bold, bright, and honest, and she was encouraged to keep painting.

What inspired her?

As Frida's health improved she started to dress in long, brightly colored skirts, in elaborate head dresses, and to wear lots of jewelry, in a traditional Mexican style. She was also inspired to use ideas from Mexican folk art in her paintings. Frida's paintings attracted worldwide attention and she has become an internationally-recognized artist. Her paintings speak of what it's like to be in pain, to be a woman, and to be Mexican.

Self-PORTRAIT

MOST OF FRIDA'S PAINTINGS WERE SELF-PORTRAITS, AND CONTAINED A LOT OF SYMBOLISM WHICH WAS PERSONAL TO HER. DRAW YOUR OWN SELF-PORTRAIT BELOW, INCLUDING IMAGES THAT ARE SYMBOLIC TO YOU AND YOUR LIFE.

SYMBOLISM OFTEN SEEN IN FRIDA'S PAINTINGS

Roots = growth but also being trapped in a particular place and situation

Trees = hope and strength

Hair = femininity

Medical imagery = pain from her accident and injuries

GRACE O'Malley

Irish pirate

Circa 1530 - 1603

Grace O'Malley (or Gráinne Ní Mháille in Irish) was born to the Ní Mháille clan in Ireland. The Ní Mháilles were fearless seamen and Grace wanted in on the action. She begged her dad to let her go out on the waves, but he refused, making up a ridiculous argument about her long hair getting stuck in the ship's rigging. Grace was not the kind of girl to let a hairstyle get in her way, so she took a knife and chopped off her hair. Her dad didn't have much of an argument left after that, so she joined the crew.

When her father died Grace inherited his shipping business. She was in charge of 20 ships and hundreds of men. At this time Ireland was ruled by dozens of clans, and Grace repeatedly commanded her fleet in successful raids on rival clans. Her crew would also attack ships that were crossing the bay and demand a fee for safe passage (which is a roundabout way of saying they were pirates).

Grace was a fearless fighter and a fearsome foe. When a rival clan, the MacMahons of Ballyvoy, killed one of her friends, Grace attacked their castle, killed the murderers, and took the castle for herself. She was not someone you'd want to mess with. When her son and brother were taken captive by the English, Grace sailed to England to ask Queen Elizabeth I for their release. Elizabeth was impressed by the pirate queen and agreed to her request on the condition that she stop attacking English ships.

WHAT'S YOUR PIRATE FLAG?

TOSS A COIN TO FIND OUT WHAT
YOUR PIRATE LIFE WOULD BE LIKE.

What's your emblem?

Heads: A unicorn   Tails: A mermaid

What's the color theme?

Heads: Pink and blue

Tails: Black and white

What's the border?

Heads: Stars   Tails: Diamonds

DRAW YOUR FLAG HERE:

WHAT'S YOUR PIRATE NAME?

Now toss the coin to decide the
four parts of your pirate name.

First name:

Heads: Rusty   Tails: Shudders

Second name:

Heads: Mc   Tails: O'

Third name:

Heads: Swindle   Tails: Bludger

Fourth name:

Heads: Skull   Tails: Bottom

NOW PUT IT ALL TOGETHER:

Hatshepsut

Egyptian pharaoh

Circa 1507 – 1458 BCE

HATSHEPSUT RULED EGYPT FOR 20 YEARS. SHE BROUGHT PEACE AND WEALTH TO HER PEOPLE.

HATSHEPSUT ESTABLISHED TRADE NETWORKS AND OVERSAW EXPEDITIONS TO FAR OFF LANDS. A TRADING EXPEDITION TO THE LAND OF PUNT BROUGHT BACK VAST RICHES INCLUDING:

* **frankincense**

(she charred the frankincense, which is a resin, and ground it into "kohl" eyeliner—the first recorded use of this)

* **live myrrh trees**

(the first recorded transplantation of foreign trees)

* ebony   * leopard skins
* gold   * incense

HATSHEPSUT USED THE WEALTH FROM THESE TRIPS TO FUND IMPRESSIVE, HIGH-QUALITY BUILDING PROJECTS. THESE INCLUDED:

* **Karnak's Red Chapel**

which was carved with stones that depicted events from her life

* **Twin obelisks**

at the entrance to the temple of Karnak. These were the tallest in the world at that time.

* The cavernous, underground **temple of Pakhet**

* An enormous, architecturally groundbreaking **memorial temple at Deir el-Bahri**

* **Hundreds of statues**

Hatshepsut is considered by experts to be one of the most successful pharaohs of all time. She achieved more than any other, which is so important because at the time it was very unusual to have a female pharaoh at all.

Design a death mask

Ancient Egyptians liked to immortalize themselves in various artworks—sphinxes, death masks, and sarcophagi, just to name a few. The sphinx of Hatshepsut portrays the pharaoh with the powerful, muscular body of a lion and a human head. She wears a traditional headcloth and royal beard to symbolize her power.

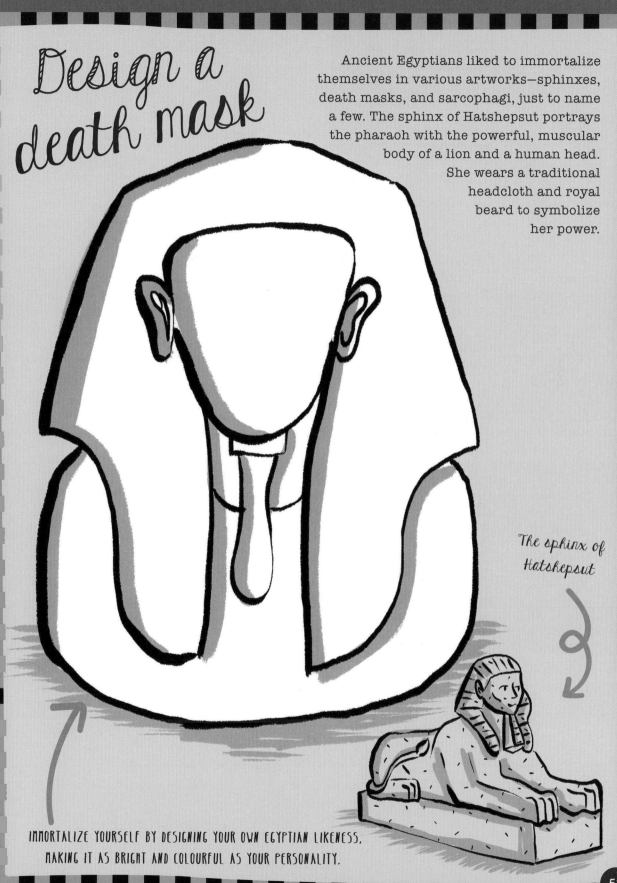

The sphinx of Hatshepsut

IMMORTALIZE YOURSELF BY DESIGNING YOUR OWN EGYPTIAN LIKENESS, MAKING IT AS BRIGHT AND COLOURFUL AS YOUR PERSONALITY.

Helen KELLER

AMERICAN ACTIVIST

1890 - 1968

When Helen Keller was just 19 months old she suffered from an illness that left her blind and deaf. Frustrated that she was unable to communicate, she used to have huge temper tantrums and would throw herself to the ground, kicking and screaming. A brilliant teacher named Anne Sullivan started to work with Helen and taught her how to communicate in other ways.

By the age of 21
Helen had mastered:

- finger spelling
- speaking
- TOUCH-LIP READING
- typing
- BRAILLE

She could communicate in:

FRENCH   GERMAN   LATIN   GREEK

HELEN USED HER EXPERIENCES TO HELP OTHER PEOPLE UNDERSTAND DISABILITIES AND CAMPAIGNED THROUGHOUT HER LIFE TO IMPROVE THE WELFARE OF DEAF AND BLIND PEOPLE.

Other amazing things about Helen:

- She was the first deaf-blind person to earn a bachelor of arts degree.
- Her birthday on June 27 is honored as Helen Keller Day in the state of Pennsylvania.
- She campaigned for women's suffrage, labor rights, socialism, antimilitarism, and other causes.
- In 1971 she was inducted into the Alabama Women's Hall of Fame.

GET IN TOUCH

Imagine waking up in a country where no one understands anything you say and you can't understand them. What if you have something really important to say? Write down three words to describe how you might feel.

1.

2.

3.

Helen Keller used her sense of touch to communicate. Can you communicate a message to a friend this way? Put blindfolds on so that you can't cheat, stay silent, and use only your sense of touch to pass on your message. Below are some messages you can try, but you can make up your own.

YOU'RE MY BEST FRIEND.   SHALL WE WATCH A MOVIE?   I LOVE PIZZA.

After you've tried this challenge, write down your thoughts about how it went. Was it easier or harder than you expected?

Helen Keller

Helen's signature

Hua
MULAN

华

HUA = FLOWER

木兰

MULAN = MAGNOLIA

ANCIENT
Chinese
warrior

Circa
420 - 589

Hua Mulan is a legendary and fearless girl first described in an ancient poem, "The Ballad of Mulan." The tale also inspired the Disney movie, *Mulan*. The ballad tells how the Chinese army called on one male from each family to serve in the war, but Mulan bravely volunteered instead. Her brother was just a child and her father was old and weak, whereas Mulan was strong, practiced kung fu and archery, and was skilled with a sword. Being an incredible horse-rider and epic fighter, she survived 12 years of battles.

When the war ended Mulan was offered an important job and lots of money as a reward, but all she asked for was a horse to carry her home. When she got there, she greeted her happy family, changed out of her warrior clothes, and went to meet her army comrades. They were amazed to see the soldier they had been fighting alongside all this time was a girl, but it didn't change their strong friendships.

THE BALLAD OF YOU

Write a poem about something in your life
you are proud to have achieved. Remember
that not all poems need to rhyme.

HYPATIA

GREEK MATHEMATICIAN,

astronomer

and philosopher

CIRCA 355 - 415

WHO WAS THIS AWESOME WOMAN?

Hypatia was a Greek living in Alexandria, Egypt, then a part of the Eastern Roman Empire. She had a powerful intellect and when she spoke, people listened. In her time she was the world's leading mathematician and astronomer. She was able to make very complicated things, such as how to design an astrolabe (a kind of portable astronomical calculator), understandable to ordinary people. Huge crowds of loyal students came to hear her teachings.

GREAT! ... OR WAS IT?

At this time, Christians, Jews, and the state were involved in a bitter religious conflict. The Christians saw Hypatia as a problem—if only she would stop going on about science and philosophy then people would be more likely to accept the religious teachings of the church. Hypatia became the focus of riots between the Christians and those who wanted to defend Alexandria as a seat of learning and culture.

WHO WON THE BATTLE?

Sadly, Hypatia was murdered by a group of Christian monks. Hypatia's death came to be seen as the end of the ancient Greek and Roman world. To this day she remains a symbol of reason and learning in the face of ignorance, and the need for tolerance of many types of ideas.

Feeling
PHILOSOPHICAL

PHILOSOPHY IS THE STUDY OF QUESTIONS ABOUT LIFE: WHO ARE WE? WHY ARE WE HERE? WHAT IS RIGHT AND WHAT IS WRONG? HYPATIA THOUGHT HARD ABOUT THESE QUESTIONS. READ THE QUESTIONS ON THIS PAGE AND JOT DOWN ANY THOUGHTS YOU HAVE.

What is the difference between virtual reality and the real world?

IF A TREE FALLS OVER IN A FOREST AND THERE'S NO ONE AROUND TO HEAR IT, DOES IT STILL MAKE A SOUND?

Are there ever times when you should tell a lie?

Can you lie to yourself?

Is math something humans created or something we discovered?

If everyone thinks something is true, does that make it true?

"PHILOSOPHY" IS FROM THE GREEK WORD "PHILOSOPHIA."

Philo = Love   Sophia = Wisdom

J.K. ROWLING
British novelist

Born 1965

"We do not need magic to change the world. We carry all the power we need inside ourselves already: we have the power to imagine better."

Jo's pathway to magic

As a young girl, Jo wrote fantasy stories to tell her sister. At six she wrote a book about a rabbit called Rabbit, and at 11 she wrote a novel about seven cursed diamonds and the people who owned them.

Jo wanted to write a book about a magical world, an idea she'd had many years ago while waiting on a delayed train. She worked hard to fit in writing whenever she could. She even wrote in cafes, in short bursts, when her baby daughter was sleeping.

But she was unhappy as a teenager. Her mom was often unwell and she didn't get on with her dad.

Life was difficult for Jo as an adult too. She felt like her life was a mess. She was a single mom with no job and no money.

Twelve publishers rejected her manuscript, until one day it was finally accepted and *Harry Potter and the Philosopher's Stone* was published.

GO, JO!

Imagine how Jo must have felt when she received all those rejection letters. It takes courage to keep trying when it feels like everything's going wrong. Can you think of five words or sentences to describe how Jo must have felt?

1. _____
2. _____
3. _____
4. _____
5. _____

Magic millions

WHAT'S YOUR MILLIONAIRE BOOK IDEA? JOT DOWN SOME IDEAS FOR CHARACTERS, THEME, AND PLOT.

Abracadabra! Five years later Jo was a bestselling author and a multi-millionaire. She was even richer than the Queen of England!

The *Harry Potter* series is now the bestselling book series in history and has won many awards.

Jo has never forgotten how hard things were for her. She supports a charity called Gingerbread which helps single parents, and she gives loads of time and money to other charities.

Jane GOODALL

BRITISH CONSERVATIONIST, ETHOLOGIST, AND PRIMATOLOGIST

Born 1934

Age 4
Jane hides for hours in a hen house to study the hens and find out where eggs come from.

Age 8
Jane discovers her love of animals by reading the *Doctor Dolittle* books and watching *Tarzan*.

Age 10
Jane dreams of traveling to Africa to watch and write about animals. Her mother tells her to work hard and never give up.

Age 18
Jane leaves school, but can't afford to go to college. She works as a waitress and saves enough money to travel to a friend's farm in Kenya.

Age 26
In Kenya Jane meets some famous scientists and studies chimpanzees. She discovers that chimpanzees use tools, eat meat, can understand human emotions, and can even learn to communicate using sign language.

Today, Jane still travels the world speaking about threats facing chimpanzees and urges us to take action for all living things.

HAPPY

Move your hands in circles in front of your chest.

SAD

Move your hands down in front of your face.

EAT

Mime putting food to your mouth.

LEARN THE LANGUAGE

This is the sign language Jane taught to a chimpanzee called Washoe. Washoe then taught some of these signs to her son Loulis.

MUSIC

Move your right hand as if you're conducting an orchestra.

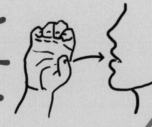

DRINK

Mime drinking from a cup.

An idea begins

When Jessica was a young girl she lived on a boat and was home-schooled by her parents. One day, Jessica's mom read her a bedtime story written by a boy who had sailed around the world all by himself. The book planted an idea in Jessica's head.

JESSICA Watson

AUSTRALIAN SAILOR

BORN 1993

A PLAN IN action

Over the next few years Jessica made it her mission to learn everything she could about boats. She completed thousands of miles of sailing experience and gained qualifications in subjects such as radio operation and yacht master theory. She carefully planned an exciting trip: she would sail around the world without stopping and without receiving any supplies on to the boat.

Sailing TO SUCCESS

At the age of 16 Jessica set off in a yacht called *Ella's Pink Lady*. The route took her across four oceans and through some of the world's most treacherous waters—huge waves even tipped her boat right over, but Jessica never gave up. Seven months later she arrived back in Sydney Harbour to a hero's welcome. She'd done it!

AN OCEAN OF SUPPORT

Many people said that the journey was too risky for a teenager, but Jessica's parents believed in their daughter and did everything they could to help her make her dream come true.

steps to SUCCESS

When Jessica arrived back in Sydney Harbour, the Prime Minister of Australia described her as a hero. Jessica disagreed, and said she was just a regular girl who had worked hard.

JESSICA'S YACHT, ELLA'S PINK LADY

There are many steps you might go through in the process of achieving a goal. Think of four goals that you would like to achieve over the coming year and write each down next to the staircases below. Which step are you on at the moment? Color in that step, and each time you go up a step toward achieving your goal, color it in.

goal
....

YES! I did it!

| I WILL DO IT |
| I CAN DO IT |
| I'LL TRY AND DO IT |
| HOW DO I DO IT? |
| I WANT TO DO IT |
| I CAN'T DO IT |
| I WON'T DO IT |

Which step have you reached today?

goal
....

YES! I did it!

| I WILL DO IT |
| I CAN DO IT |
| I'LL TRY AND DO IT |
| HOW DO I DO IT? |
| I WANT TO DO IT |
| I CAN'T DO IT |
| I WON'T DO IT |

Which step have you reached today?

goal
....

YES! I did it!

| I WILL DO IT |
| I CAN DO IT |
| I'LL TRY AND DO IT |
| HOW DO I DO IT? |
| I WANT TO DO IT |
| I CAN'T DO IT |
| I WON'T DO IT |

Which step have you reached today?

goal
....

YES! I did it!

| I WILL DO IT |
| I CAN DO IT |
| I'LL TRY AND DO IT |
| HOW DO I DO IT? |
| I WANT TO DO IT |
| I CAN'T DO IT |
| I WON'T DO IT |

Which step have you reached today?

Kate Sheppard

LEADER OF NEW ZEALAND'S WOMEN'S SUFFRAGE MOVEMENT

1847 – 1934

KATE WAS BORN IN LIVERPOOL, ENGLAND, BUT WHEN SHE WAS 21 SHE AND HER FAMILY MOVED TO CHRISTCHURCH IN NEW ZEALAND.

Things Kate didn't like about Christchurch:

WOMEN HAD TO WEAR TIGHT CORSETS.

Children were allowed to buy alcohol.

Women weren't allowed to have jobs.

Women weren't allowed to vote.

Something had to be done

Kate was a tireless worker. She cycled around Christchurch (gasp, a woman on a bicycle!) delivering pamphlets and making speeches about the need for women to vote. Some people were very angry about this and said that she should stop meddling in "men's affairs" and get back to her housework. But thousands and thousands of people agreed with Kate and signed petitions that were taken to parliament. At first Kate's petitions failed, but she didn't give up and in 1893 a "monster" petition signed by more than 30,000 supporters was successful. New Zealand became the first country in the world to grant women the right to vote. Kate had given hope and inspiration to suffragettes across the globe.

WHY VOTE?

Below are five reasons to get out there and vote when you are old enough. Number the reasons by importance, number 1 being what you think is the most important reason and number 5 being the least important.

☐	☐	☐	☐	☐
IT GIVES YOU THE POWER TO CREATE CHANGE.	IT ENCOURAGES POLITICIANS TO WORK FOR YOUNG ADULTS.	MANY CAMPAIGNS LIKE KATE'S HAVE TAKEN PLACE TO GIVE YOU THE RIGHT TO VOTE.	POLITICIANS CAN SOLVE PROBLEMS IN YOUR LOCAL AREA AND FOR LOCAL PEOPLE.	IT WILL BE YOUR MONEY THE GOVERNMENT IS SPENDING—OR CUTTING.

Design a badge to promote women's rights that Kate would have worn with pride.

LELLA Lombardi

Italian racing CAR DRIVER

1941 - 1992

AGE 4
Lella makes toy cars from things she finds in her mother's sewing box and races them around the kitchen.

AGE 8
SHE DECIDES THAT SHE WANTS TO BE A RACING DRIVER WHEN SHE GROWS UP.

AGE 15
Lella spends her free time racing motorbikes with other teenagers in her village.

AGE 18
She enters her first real motor car race.

AGE 34
Lella is approached by March Engineering Ltd to join their Grand Prix Team. She becomes the first woman in 17 years (and the second ever) to compete on the Formula One Grand Prix circuit.

AGE 24
Lella buys a second-hand Formula Monza 500 that she fixes up and drives in races.

AGE 34
Lella becomes the first woman ever to score points in a Grand Prix when she comes 6th in the 1975 Spanish Grand Prix. It's an eventful race in which the rear wing of a competitor's car breaks off and flies into the crowd. Five spectators are killed and the driver suffers broken bones. Racing driving used to be a really dangerous sport.

AGE 50
LELLA DIES IN MILAN. A STATUE COMMEMORATING HER CAN BE SEEN IN HER BIRTHPLACE OF FRUGAROLO.

ON FORM FOR FORMULA 1

If you want to make it as a professional racing car driver you'll need super-fast reaction times. Follow these instructions to make your own reaction timer and put your reflexes to the test.

1. Take a piece of card sized 8in x 2in. From the bottom of the card, working upwards, write the time in milliseconds at the inch distances shown below.

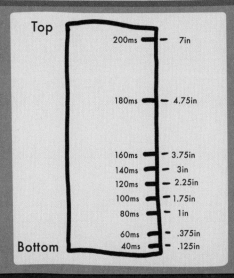

Top	
200ms	7in
180ms	4.75in
160ms	3.75in
140ms	3in
120ms	2.25in
100ms	1.75in
80ms	1in
60ms	.375in
40ms	.125in
Bottom	

Lella making history at the 1975 Spanish Grand Prix

2. Ask a friend to hold the card at the top, and position your hand underneath ready to catch it with your thumb and forefinger as soon as they drop it. Ask your friend to drop the card without warning. Catch it as quickly as you can.

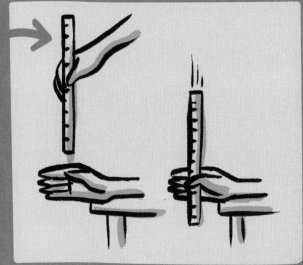

3. Read your time from the side of the card at the point you caught it. The lower your score, the faster your reaction time and the more suitable you are for a career as a racing driver. Keep practicing and try to improve on your personal best.

MAE
Jemison

...ICAN ASTRONAUT

BORN 1956

Things Mae LOVED as a little girl:

★ SPACE   ★ THE STARS   ★ DINOSAURS
★ ADVENTURING

But ... she wondered why there were no female astronauts. Well, she'll just have to become one!

Things Mae was GREAT AT IN SCHOOL:

★ SCIENCE   ★ DANCING

★ LANGUAGES (RUSSIAN, SWAHILI, AND JAPANESE)

Seems like Mae was talented at just about everything.

Things Mae did during COLLEGE and afterward:

★ STUDIED CHEMICAL ENGINEERING

★ QUALIFIED AS A DOCTOR AND WORKED AS A GP

★ SERVED AS A MEDICAL OFFICER IN THE PEACE CORPS IN WEST AFRICA WHERE SHE HELPED TO IMPROVE HEALTH CARE AND WORKED ON SEVERAL RESEARCH PROJECTS

Seriously, is there anything Mae can't do?

Things Mae did with NASA and beyond:

★ APPLIED TO NASA'S ASTRONAUT PROGRAM—AND SUCCEEDED!

★ BECAME THE FIRST AFRICAN-AMERICAN WOMAN TO GO INTO SPACE

★ FOUNDED HER OWN TECHNOLOGY COMPANY

★ STARTED THE EARTH WE SHARE PROJECT, A SCIENCE CAMP WHERE CHILDREN WORK TO FIND SOLUTIONS TO THE WORLD'S PROBLEMS

★ BECAME PRESIDENT OF THE 100 YEAR STARSHIP, A PROJECT TO DEVELOP TRAVEL TO OTHER STAR SYSTEMS

We love you, Mae!

To infinity and beyond

Things I loved when I was little:

- -

- -

- -

- -

- -

Things I am great at in school:

- -

- -

- -

- -

- -

Things I want to do after
I finish school:

- -

- -

- -

- -

- -

Things I want to achieve in life:

- -

- -

- -

- -

- -

What would be the best things about traveling to space?

- -

- -

- -

- -

ON HER FIRST TRIP TO
SPACE, MAE
TRAVELED ON THE
SPACE SHUTTLE
ENDEAVOUR.

MALALA YOUSAFZAI

PAKISTANI ACTIVIST

BORN 1997

"There is no greater weapon than knowledge."

MALALA HAD A FUN CHILDHOOD, PLAYING OUTDOORS AND LEARNING ABOUT THE WORLD FROM BOOKS. BUT IN 2007 THE TALIBAN, A STRICT ISLAMIST POLITICAL GROUP, TOOK CONTROL OF THE AREA IN WHICH MALALA LIVED. THEY BANNED MANY THINGS.

BANNED BY THE TALIBAN:

WATCHING TELEVISION	PLAYING MUSIC	CELEBRATING NEW YEAR	GIRLS GOING TO SCHOOL	WOMEN LAUGHING LOUDLY

Malala wrote an online blog about how it felt to live under the Taliban. News agencies around the world became interested in her story. Malala fought publicly for the right for girls to go to school. The Taliban didn't like this at all and tried to murder her. She had just taken an exam and was riding home on a bus when a masked gunman shot her in the head. Miraculously, Malala didn't die. After being transferred to various hospitals, she settled in England for treatment and made a full recovery.

WHAT MALALA HAS ACHIEVED SINCE:

SHE CONTINUES TO FIGHT FOR EDUCATION AND HAS MET WITH HEADS OF STATE ALL OVER THE WORLD TO PROMOTE HER CAUSE.

SHE PUBLISHED HER MEMOIR IN 2013.

IN 2014 SHE BECAME THE YOUNGEST EVER WINNER OF THE NOBEL PEACE PRIZE.

SHE OPENED A SCHOOL FOR SYRIAN REFUGEE GIRLS IN LEBANON, IN 2015.

SHE WAS ACCEPTED INTO OXFORD UNIVERSITY IN 2017 TO STUDY PHILOSOPHY, POLITICS, AND ECONOMICS.

Make MALALA proud

Malala fights to ensure girls have the right to go to school.
What are your top five things about going to school?

1. _____

2. _____

3. _____

4. _____

5. _____

WHAT SUBJECTS DO YOU WANT TO CONTINUE OR START STUDYING WHEN YOU'RE OLDER?

_____

_____

_____

_____

How do you think study helps you to help other people?

_____

_____

_____

_____

Maria
CALLAS

GREEK-AMERICAN
opera singer

1923 - 1977

Age 3 — Maria feels that her mother loves her beautiful, graceful sister more than she loves her. Maria only feels loved when she sings.

Age 5 — Maria's mother starts making her perform for money. Maria hates it and just wants to be left alone to play and have fun like a normal child.

Age 13 — Maria's mother tries to enroll her in the Athens Conservatoire, a famous music school, but Maria fails the audition. They say that her voice isn't good enough.

Age 14 — A teacher, Maria Trivella, hears Maria sing: her voice swirls and flares like a flame. This is talent! The teacher agrees to help Maria train her voice.

Age 16 — Maria auditions again for the Athens Conservatoire. This time she is accepted. There, she increases her vocal range, developing her high notes and discovering her low "chest" notes. She is like an athlete training her voice.

Age 18 — Maria makes her professional debut. The other performers are jealous of Maria's incredible voice and say mean things about her. Maria doesn't let it hold her back.

And beyond ... — Maria performs professionally for the next 24 years and stars in nearly 50 operas. The passion that Maria brings to the stage helps the audience to really feel the joy, pain, happiness, and anger of the characters she plays. Maria becomes known as La Davina—"The Divine."

BEL CANTO!

Bel Canto means "beautiful singing." Want to sing like Maria? The first step is to get your singing posture right.

The head is pulling your spine up. The body feels long and tall.

THE CHIN IS PARALLEL TO THE FLOOR.

Shoulders are down and relaxed.

THE CHEST IS OPEN AND FLEXIBLE.

The back is lengthened and wide.

HIPS ARE IN ALIGNMENT WITH THE SPINE, NECK, AND SHOULDERS.

Knees are relaxed and not locked.

Feet are shoulder width apart and weight is distributed evenly.

NEXT, WARM UP YOUR VOICE ...

The lip bubble:

This is just like blowing a raspberry. Put your fingers into your cheeks near your chin. Keep your lips closed but relaxed and blow air through them.

The elevator:

Using an "Ahhhhh" sound, start on a low note and smoothly slide right up to your highest note and back down again.

YOU'RE READY! CHOOSE A SONG AND SING YOUR HEART OUT.

Maria
CORAZON
Aquino
1933 – 2009

Former President of the Philippines

WHAT HAPPENED TO CORY?

When Maria, or Cory as she was known to her friends, was 22, she married a young politician called Benigno. They settled into life raising their five children at home. At that time the Philippines was being run by a corrupt dictator called Ferdinand Marcos. Cory's husband spoke out publicly against Marcos. Marcos had Benigno jailed for 8 years, exiled to the USA, and then killed on his return.

WHAT DID CORY DO ABOUT IT?

Cory stepped up to lead demonstrations and protests against Marcos. People all over the Philippines came to see her speak. She became the head of the anti-Marcos movement. Marcos could see that his grip on the country was loosening.

HOW DID MARCOS REACT?

Hoping to justify his power, Marcos asked everyone in the country to vote on who they thought should be president. They voted for Cory, but Marcos rigged the votes and claimed that he had won.

DID CORY COME TO THE RESCUE?

Yes! Cory organized strikes and encouraged everyone to stop using the businesses owned by Marcos. These popular, peaceful demonstrations came to be known as the "People Power Revolution." Marcos was forced to give in and Cory became President of the Philippines. She brought freedom and democracy back to the country and improved the lives of thousands of people.

We are all born free

THE UNIVERSAL DECLARATION OF HUMAN RIGHTS STATES THAT WE ARE ALL BORN FREE AND EQUAL; YOU HAVE THE RIGHT TO HAVE AN EDUCATION, TO HAVE A REST FROM WORK, TO BELONG TO A COUNTRY.

Imagine that you are the president of your own country. What rights do you think are important for the people of your country to have? Write one idea for each of the sun rays below. This sun symbol is from the Filipino flag.

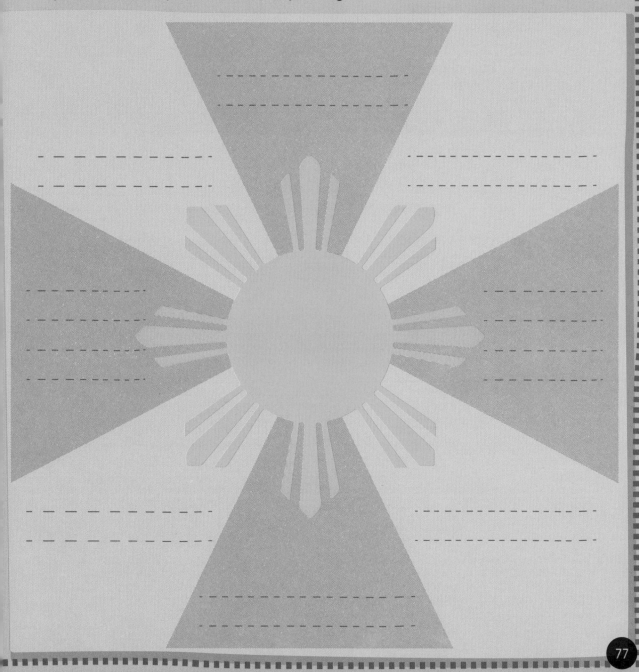

ITALIAN DOCTOR

AND EDUCATOR

1870 - 1952

Maria Montessori

How did Maria stand up for herself?

Maria's home town was Chiravelle in Italy. When she was a teenager she attended a boys' school where she could study math and science, and went on to become Italy's first female doctor.

How did she make a difference?

Maria spent a lot of time working with children who had disabilities. She saw that all children have an almost effortless ability to learn new skills—they just have to be allowed to get on with it. She decided to leave her job as a doctor and focus on developing a new kind of school. In 1907 Maria set up the first Casa dei Bambini, or "Children's House."

How were these schools different?

Maria got rid of boring teachers who bossed children around. She filled the classrooms with exciting activities and the children could choose what they wanted to do. Maria told the teachers that their job was to get to know each child and make sure that they had everything they needed to be able to learn.

Did it work out?

The Casa dei Bambini was a huge success and Maria traveled all over the world telling people about her new way of teaching. By 1925, more than 1,000 of her schools had opened in America, and there are now 22,000 Montessori schools all over the globe.

MARVELOUS MONTESSORI

It's not just Montessori schools that use Maria's ideas—teachers all over the world have changed the way they do things. Think back to the school you went to when you were very young (probably a pre-school). Can you spot Maria's influences?

MARIA SWAPPED ...	FOR ...	WHAT WAS IT LIKE AT YOUR SCHOOL?
Big, heavy furniture	Light furniture that children could move by themselves	
Making children sit at desks all day	Letting children move inside and outside as they pleased	
Telling children what to do	Providing all sorts of activities and letting children choose what they want to do	
Doing things for children	Allowing children to do things for themselves	
Writing with a pen and paper	Using different kinds of materials such as writing in a sand tray or using letters cut out of card	
Fixed lesson times	Letting children work at an activity for as long as they wanted	
Classes of children all the same age	Mixed-age classes so students could learn from older children and help younger ones	

Polish PHYSICIST and CHEMIST

Marie Curie

1867 – 1934

Why Marie is marvelous

She won not one but two Nobel Prizes. One for physics in 1903 for discovering the chemical elements radium and polonium, and one for chemistry in 1911 for her research into radioactivity.

MARIE CURIE'S DISCOVERIES IN THE FIELD OF RADIOACTIVITY WERE CRUCIAL IN DEVELOPING TODAY'S TREATMENT OF CANCER AND HAVE SAVED MILLIONS OF LIVES.

She was the first woman to teach at the Sorbonne University in Paris.

During World War I, she created a fleet of mobile X-ray units (nicknamed Petits Curies), which she often drove to the frontline herself. Her invention helped to save the lives of over a million soldiers.

THE INTERNATIONAL RED CROSS MADE HER HEAD OF ITS RADIOLOGICAL SERVICE AND SHE HELD TRAINING COURSES FOR DOCTORS.

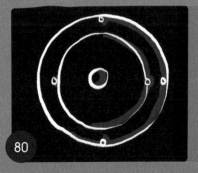

WHAT IS RADIOACTIVITY?

An atom is made up of two main parts, the nucleus and the electrons. Some materials are radioactive because the nucleus of each atom is unstable and can decay by giving out nuclear radiation. When radiation comes into contact with living cells it can damage them and cause harm, such as causing the cell to turn cancerous.

Innovation STATION

Marie Curie was a scientist and an inventor. She looked around at the world and saw what was needed, then went ahead and invented a solution to the problem. Is there a problem that could be fixed by a new invention?

Choose a problem to solve:

- Socks always getting holes in the toes
- Plants dying from lack of water when you're on vacation
- Your phone battery dying when you don't have your charger with you
- Wildlife not being able to safely cross the road

What could you invent to solve the problem?

....

....

....

....

Who would benefit from your invention?

....

....

....

....

Draw a picture of your invention here:

Could you actually make your invention? Maybe you can follow in Marie's footsteps and change the world.

British fossil hunter and paleontologist

Mary had a stall on the seafront with her dad, selling the shells, stones, and "dragon's teeth" they found on the beach.

Made many important finds in Jurassic marine fossil beds.

Born and lived in the seaside town of Lyme Regis in England

Mary ANNING

1799 – 1847

HER FINDINGS CONTRIBUTED TO IMPORTANT CHANGES IN SCIENTIFIC THINKING ABOUT THE HISTORY OF LIVING THINGS AND THE EARTH.

Mary rarely went to school, but she could read and write and taught herself all about geology and anatomy.

She discovered the first complete fossil of an Ichthyosaurus at age 12.

SCIENTISTS FROM AROUND THE WORLD BECAME INTERESTED IN MARY'S FINDS, AND TRAVELED TO MEET HER.

Defying death

WHEN MARY WAS A BABY SHE WAS AT A HORSE SHOW IN A THUNDERSTORM. WHEN LIGHTNING STRUCK, THE WOMAN THAT WAS HOLDING BABY MARY DIED, BUT MARY WAS UNHURT. IN FACT, HER FAMILY SAID SHE HAD BEEN A SICKLY BABY BEFORE THE EVENT, BUT FROM THEN ON WAS FULL OF SPARK!

Dragon's teeth

200 MILLION YEARS AGO, MARY'S HOME TOWN WAS BENEATH THE SEA. THE "DRAGON'S TEETH" THAT MARY FOUND WERE THE FOSSILIZED REMAINS OF ANIMALS THAT SWAM IN THE DEEP ALL THAT TIME AGO.

Identifying fossils

Correctly identifying fossils isn't easy. They are often only partially complete or can be all scrambled up. You need to be a real expert—like Mary. Imagine you have found these four fossils below and try to match them up with the real-life creatures underneath.

Fossil 1

Fossil 2

Fossil 3

Fossil 4

CREATURE 1

CREATURE 2

CREATURE 3

CREATURE 4

The plesiosaur fossil discovered by Mary, now on display at the Natural History Museum in London

ANSWERS: Fossil 1 = CREATURE 3, Fossil 2 = CREATURE 1, Fossil 3 = CREATURE 4, Fossil 4 = CREATURE 2

Mary SHERMAN Morgan

1921 – 2004

AMERICAN ROCKET SCIENTIST

Until the age of 8, Mary spent her days working on her family's farm, but then the authorities noticed that she wasn't going to school and said she had to go. While Mary was studying chemistry at college during World War II, America developed a shortage of chemists. She was offered a job at a factory, but she didn't know what the factory made, only that she would be required to get "top secret" security clearance. Mysterious! Short on money, Mary took the job anyway and it turned out that she would be making explosives for the military.

After the war, Mary joined a company called North American Aviation. Her job was to calculate the expected performance of new rocket fuels. There were 900 male engineers there and only one woman: Mary. Almost all of the engineers had a college degree, but Mary didn't. Even so she was the best rocket scientist in the company.

When the Soviet Union successfully launched the first satellite into space, the United States were desperate to catch up in the "space race." The problem was that they didn't have a rocket fuel that was powerful enough. They turned to North American Aviation for help.

Mary worked on the problem for months, conducting research and doing calculations. She designed a new fuel called "Hydyne." On January 31,1958, the United States used Hydyne to boost their first satellite, Explorer 1, into space. Thanks to Mary, America was back in the space race!

Make your own
ROCKET FUEL

Fuel propels a rocket upwards with a chemical reaction. Try this chemical reaction below to watch how two substances interact together. It might not launch a rocket, but it can be dramatic, so stand well back and only do it outside.

You will need:

- A large plastic bottle of diet soda
- A packet of mints with a hard outer shell and a soft center
- An 8.5in x 11in piece of paper or card
- A 4in x 4in square of cardboard
- Sticky tape

1

TAKE THE PIECE OF PAPER OR CARD AND ROLL IT UP INTO A TUBE. THE TUBE SHOULD BE THE SAME WIDTH AS THE TOP OF YOUR BOTTLE. FIX THE TUBE WITH STICKY TAPE.

2

TAKE THE LID OFF THE BOTTLE. PLACE THE SMALL SQUARE OF CARDBOARD OVER THE TOP OF THE BOTTLE.

3

PUT THE TUBE ON TOP OF THE FLAT PIECE OF CARDBOARD AND FILL IT WITH MINTS.

4

HOLD THE TUBE OF MINTS IN PLACE WITH ONE HAND AND, IN ONE QUICK MOVEMENT, REMOVE THE SMALLER PIECE OF CARDBOARD WITH THE OTHER HAND. THE MINTS SHOULD FALL INTO THE BOTTLE. QUICKLY GRAB THE EMPTY TUBE AND MOVE AWAY.

5

STAND BACK!

Launch of Explorer 1

WHAT'S HAPPENING?

Soda is full of a gas called carbon dioxide. When the mints fall into the drink, they encourage the carbon dioxide to create large bubbles. The bubbles only want to go in one direction—up! The narrow neck of the bottle forces the liquid to speed up on its way out. All of this combined creates a spectacular fizzy fountain.

85

MAYA Angelou

AMERICAN AUTHOR AND ACTIVIST

1928 - 2014

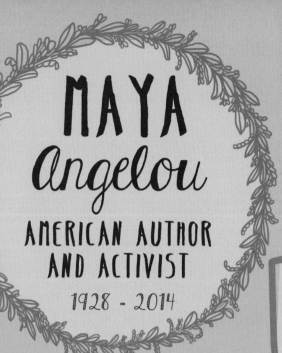

Age 7

Sadly Maya was badly abused. She spoke out about the abuse and her abuser was murdered. As a result, Maya refused to speak for the next five years. She understood that words could be powerful, and she worried about her words harming others.

Age 12

Maya became friends with a teacher called Mrs. Flowers. Mrs. Flowers introduced Maya to books and poetry and helped her to find the courage to speak.

Age 26

Maya began singing and dancing professionally in the clubs around San Francisco. She toured Europe and began learning the language of every country she visited. At around the same time, she began to take writing very seriously and met many major African-American authors. She was published for the first time. Maya often wrote about her childhood. Being a black girl in America at the time Maya grew up was tough. People treated her badly just because she was black.

Age 37

Maya had befriended the human rights activist Malcom X and helped him build a new civil rights organization. Her writing had great power and she became known as the voice of the Civil Rights Movement, a movement which aimed to end racial discrimination.

THINKING OUT LOUD

Have you ever been treated differently from others in a way you consider unfair? Try to think of three examples and write them below.

1.

2.

3.

Your
VOICE

Performing or speaking out to others can be very daunting, particularly if you are shy, but it's a terrific way to get your point across and build your confidence.

Practice in front of a mirror, and pretend you are telling someone about the things you have written down above. Focus on using clear language and a strong voice.

How did you feel about "performing" your thoughts?

Age 40

Activist and leader of the Civil Rights Movement Martin Luther King Jr. asked Maya to organize a march. But King was assassinated on Maya's 40th birthday. She was devastated. Her friends encouraged her to write to help her through her grief. Over the following years Maya wrote many books, poems, plays, and essays that remind people that everyone deserves to be treated equally, regardless of their gender or the color of their skin.

What instrument DID MELBA PLAY?

When Melba was seven years old, a traveling music store came to her school. Melba took one look at the trombone and knew that she had to have it. Melba had a natural ear for music and learned to play the instrument without taking formal lessons. After just one year of practicing she was good enough to play solo on local radio.

Melba Liston
AMERICAN MUSICIAN
1926 - 1999

What was being a FAMOUS TROMBONIST LIKE?

Melba's incredible skill on the trombone led her to work with some of the biggest names in the jazz world: Gerald Wilson, Dizzie Gillespie, John Coltrane, and Billie Holiday. She became a famous trombonist but it was a hard time to be a woman in the music industry. Melba was ignored, abused, and discriminated against. For a while she turned her back on music and worked in education instead.

Did she ever RETURN TO MUSIC?

Yes! During the late 1950s Melba returned to the music scene as a performer, arranger and composer. This took great strength and self-belief: it was virtually unheard of for women to have this kind of career in the world of jazz music. But Melba skilfully blended African rhythms and percussion with jazz horn playing and created gorgeous arrangements for many prestigious artists of the time.

MY HAPPINESS PLAYLIST

MELBA FOUND STRENGTH AND MOTIVATION IN HER MUSIC. SHE ONCE SAID THAT THE TROMBONE SAVED HER FROM SADNESS. MAKE A HAPPINESS PLAYLIST BELOW, OF 10 SONGS THAT ALWAYS BRIGHTEN YOUR DAY.

1. _____

2. _____

3. _____

4. _____

5. _____

6. _____

7. _____

8. _____

9. _____

10. _____

Which instruments do you particularly love the sound of?

_____

_____

_____

_____

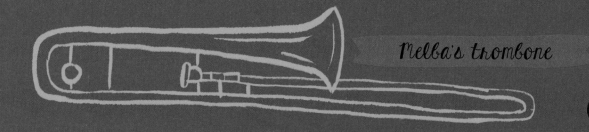

Melba's trombone

Michelle OBAMA

American lawyer, former First Lady, and humanitarian

BORN 1964

Michelle was born in Chicago, Illinois, USA. She grew up in a small apartment in South Chicago with her parents and her older brother. They were a happy family and loved playing board games such as Monopoly together.

Throughout her early life Michelle came up against people who told her not to aim too high. She experienced prejudice both because she was African American and a woman. This kind of attitude inspired Michelle to work harder and to fight for equality. Michelle's mother always told her that if there was something that could be done, she could do it.

Michelle attended Princeton University and went on to get a law degree from Harvard. While working as a lawyer she was assigned as a mentor to a young lawyer called Barack Obama. The pair fell in love, got married, and had two children together.

Michelle helped Barack campaign to become the President of the United States, and when he was voted into office she became the first African-American First Lady. She used her role to make real changes to the issues she cares about: children's health, supporting veterans, encouraging young people to stay in education after high school, and helping girls around the world go to school.

MAKE A *Change*

Imagine that, like Michelle, you have the power to draw the world's attention to the issues you care about. Think of four issues that you would focus on and the changes that could help resolve each issue. Maybe you're worried about climate change and would like to see changes in the way that people consume the earth's natural resources, or maybe you think everyone should have more time off and that weekends should be three days long.

Issue 1:
_____

Changes:
- - - - - - - - - - - - - - - -
- - - - - - - - - - - - - - - -
- - - - - - - - - - - - - - - -
- - - - - - - - - - - - - - - -

Issue 2:
_____

Changes:
- - - - - - - - - - - - - - - -
- - - - - - - - - - - - - - - -
- - - - - - - - - - - - - - - -

Issue 3:
_____

Changes:
- - - - - - - - - - - - - - - -
- - - - - - - - - - - - - - - -
- - - - - - - - - - - - - - - -
- - - - - - - - - - - - - - - -

Issue 4:
_____

Changes:
- - - - - - - - - - - - - - - -
- - - - - - - - - - - - - - - -
- - - - - - - - - - - - - - - -
- - - - - - - - - - - - - - - -

The Mirabal Sisters

The Mirabal sisters lived in the Dominican Republic at a time when a dictator called Rafael Trujillo was in power. Trujillo used secret police to control the country. Those who spoke out against him tended to disappear in suspicious circumstances.

The Mirabal sisters wanted to make a better country for their children. They distributed pamphlets that informed people about the terrible things Trujillo was doing, and gathered weapons. They became known as Las Mariposas, "The Butterflies."

Trujillo arranged for the sisters to be killed and he tried to make it look like an accident, but everyone in the country knew that he was responsible. The cowardly killings stirred the people of the Dominican Republic to action, and six months later Trujillo was assassinated by military leaders. The Mirabals' children were free to grow up in a fairer country.

Dominican activists

Patria

1924 - 1960

WITNESSED A MASSACRE AND WAS WILLING TO GIVE UP EVERYTHING TO BRING DOWN TRUJILLO.

Dedé

1925 - 2014

WAS THE ONLY SISTER NOT TO BE KILLED BY TRUJILLO. SHE RAISED HER SISTERS' SIX CHILDREN AFTER THEIR DEATHS AND SPENT THE REST OF HER LIFE HONORING THE BUTTERFLIES.

Minerva

1926 - 1960

WAS A BRILLIANT STUDENT WHO WANTED TO BECOME A LAWYER. SHE WAS PERSONALLY TARGETED BY TRUJILLO WHO WANTED HER TO BE HIS GIRLFRIEND. NO THANKS!

Maria Teresa

1935 - 1960

THE YOUNGEST SISTER, FOUGHT PASSIONATELY AGAINST TRUJILLO AND WAS UNAFRAID OF DEATH.

Battle of the BUTTERFLIES

The Mirabal sisters helped to transform the Dominican Republic from a dictatorship to a democracy. Can you draw a line to match the names of the different types of government to their descriptions? Find the answers at the bottom of the page.

1. DICTATORSHIP

2. DEMOCRACY

3. MONARCHY

4. THEOCRACY

5. ANARCHY

a. The government is elected by the people. Everyone who is eligible to vote has a say in who they want to run the country.

b. The country is run by a single leader who generally has not been elected and may use force to keep control.

c. Religious leaders run the country.

d. There is no government, so there are no laws and everyone does whatever they want.

e. A king or queen rules the country. Sometimes they have absolute power, and sometimes their control is limited by a democratically elected government.

Which type of government would you like to live under?

ANSWERS
1. B, 2. A, 3. E, 4. C, 5. D

93

Miriam MAKEBA

South African singer
and activist

1932 - 2008

When Miriam was 16 a new government in South Africa introduced a
system called apartheid. People were classified and treated differently according
to their race. Millions of people who were not white were forced to leave their homes
and move into segregated neighborhoods. They were not allowed to do the jobs,
use the buildings, or go to the events that white people were allowed to.

Miriam poured her heart and soul into her music. She sang about how it felt
to be a young black woman in apartheid South Africa. In 1959 she sang in a film
called *Come Back, Africa*, which drew the world's attention to what was going on in her
country. The government was angry and, when she tried to re-enter South Africa after
traveling in Europe and America, they took away her passport and said she couldn't return.

Miriam moved to America and recorded lots of popular songs that brought African
music to new audiences. She traveled the world telling people what was going on in
South Africa, and her music inspired hope. She became known as "Mama Africa."

Eventually the pressure on the South African government meant that the rules around
apartheid started to change, so Miriam returned to her homeland. She continued to sing and
speak out against injustice, and worked as a Goodwill Ambassador for the United Nations.

Songs for THE SOUL

Miriam understood the power of music to convey emotion and to change people's minds. Write down five songs that you find inspiring. What are they about and what do they mean to you?

Song 1

Song 2

Song 3

Song 4

Song 5

MUKAI Chiaki

BORN 1952

JAPANESE SURGEON AND ASTRONAUT

AGE 5
Mukai hears that the Russians have successfully launched the first satellite into space. She is super excited.

Age 9
She reads all about Yuri Gagarin, the first person to travel into space and return. Chiaki is amazed but never dreams that one day she too will become an astronaut.

Age 10
Mukai sees her poorly brother's life transformed by doctors. She writes an essay titled *What Will I Be In The Future?*: she wants to be a doctor—an unusual choice for a young girl growing up in 1950s Japan.

AGE 14
Mukai leaves her parents' home and moves to Tokyo to receive a higher level of education that will help her become a doctor.

AGE 31
Mukai reads an advert in a newspaper calling for scientists to apply to the Japanese Space Agency for the chance to conduct experiments in space. Wow! She applies, and is selected in 1985.

Age 25
She earns a doctorate in medicine and specializes in heart surgery. Her dream has come true.

Age 42
She blasts into space on the STS-65 Columbia Space Shuttle, and spends 15 days in space, orbiting the earth 236 times (covering 6.1 million miles). The astronauts conduct experiments about the effect of being in space on the human body. Mukai was the first Japanese woman to go into space and the first Japanese astronaut to go into space twice.

Wonderful weightlessness

Since returning from space, Mukai has worked to help people on the ground understand more about space travel. She created a national competition asking the Japanese public to finish a traditional "tanka" poem she had written about weightlessness. A ten-year-old-girl called Manami Tanno won the competition.

Tanka are five-line poems of 31 syllables split into a pattern of 5-7-5-7-7. Write your own tanka poem about weightlessness in the space below.

Niki de SAINT Phalle

1930 - 2002

French-American artist

Niki had a difficult childhood and education, and was expelled from three different schools. At one school she painted all the fig leaves on the school's classical sculptures red.

She married at the young age of 18 and began to paint shortly after. At this time it was unusual for women to make big, expressive pieces of art but Niki didn't think twice about doing things that were out of the ordinary. She created artworks by sticking objects and bags of paint into plaster. She would then shoot at the artwork, making the paint explode on to the plaster. Niki's first art exhibition was held in Switzerland when she was 26, and she continued to work as an artist from then on.

Niki used sculpture to explore the way women are seen in society. She created a series of sculptures showing women as witches, monsters, and skeletal brides. Later, her sculptures became more joyful: women were shown in dance poses and doing acrobatics.

One of Niki's sculptures was of the body of a woman, which was so big that there were all sorts of exhibits inside it. These included a 12-seat cinema, an aquarium, a milk bar inside one of the breasts, and a playground slide for children.

Niki didn't want to create art that was small and quiet—she wanted her art to be monumental!

BREAK THE RULES

WHY NOT FOLLOW IN NIKI'S FOOTSTEPS, THROW OUT THE RULEBOOK, AND CREATE YOUR OWN ORIGINAL ARTWORK? STUCK FOR AN IDEA? TRY ONE OF THESE NIKI-INSPIRED SUGGESTIONS.

Cover a bag of paint with papier-mâché then poke holes in it to let the paint drip through.

Find new and unusual materials for collage and sculpture. A woman made of cheese? OK!

Experiment with different ways of applying paint to a surface. You could drip it, blow it, throw it … anything goes!

Make an artwork out of things that have been thrown away. The bigger the better!

EXPERIMENT USING PAINT AND DIFFERENT VEGETABLES TO MAKE PRINTS. WHAT KIND OF EFFECTS CAN YOU CREATE USING CORN ON THE COB, OR LEMONS, OR APPLES?

Listen to your favorite piece of music and create an artwork inspired by what you hear.

Turn your bedroom into a giant sculpture. You could hang materials from the ceiling or use cardboard boxes to build out from the walls to create a new kind of space.

ONE OF NIKI'S WOMEN SCULPTURES, WHICH SHE CALLED NANAS

Australian author

1899 - 1996

Pamela Lyndon Travers

Pamela Lyndon Travers was born Helen Lyndon Goff. P.L. Travers was her pen name—her poems were first published when she was just a teenager. Pamela moved to England when she was 25. One day, when she was in the English countryside recovering from a serious illness, she imagined a nanny called Mary Poppins came to cheer her up. Mary Poppins blew into Pamela's imagination on a parrot-headed umbrella, carrying a carpet bag of magic and ready to change the lives of everyone who met her.

Pamela began to make up stories about the adventures of Mary Poppins. Her stories were published as a series of six books, and to this day they are loved by children all over the world.

Two of the biggest fans of the Mary Poppins books were two girls called Diane and Sharon Disney. Their dad, Walt Disney, decided to try to buy the rights to make a Mary Poppins film. Pamela didn't want her version of the story to be changed and she made Disney work hard to convince her to sell. He flew a few times from America to visit her at home in England, and paid for her to visit his studios in Los Angeles.

Eventually, after 20 years, Pamela agreed. When she saw the film, Pamela didn't know what to say. Disney suggested "supercalifragilisticexpialidocious"!

Let's go fly a kite

Kite flying features frequently in the Mary Poppins books. Doodle, design, and color the kites below, making them the most eye-catching kites in the sky.

Rosa
PARKS

AMERICAN ACTIVIST

"I DID NOT WANT TO BE MISTREATED, I DID NOT WANT TO BE DEPRIVED OF A SEAT THAT I HAD PAID FOR. IT WAS JUST TIME ..."

Rosa grew up in the city of Montgomery in Alabama. At that time the state was governed by racial segregation laws. This meant that black children had to go to different schools than white children, and weren't allowed to drink from the same drinking fountains or borrow books from the same libraries. White people could ride at the front of buses, but black people had to sit at the back, and could only sit down if no white person wanted the seat.

One day, when Rosa was 42 years old, she was taking the bus home from her job as a seamstress. The bus driver asked Rosa to give up her seat for a white person. Rosa was tired of giving in to these demands and politely said no.

Rosa's parents were former slaves, and from a young age Rosa had fought against the oppression of black people. She believed in the power of speaking out in the face of racism. Her dignified "no" to the bus driver caused a stir. She was arrested, and news of her arrest spread fast. People across Montgomery decided that they wouldn't use the buses until the law was changed.

Inspired by Rosa Parks and the Montgomery Bus Boycott, people across America took part in sit-ins, eat-ins, swim-ins, and other peaceful protests. Thousands of people joined together to demand equal rights for all people, regardless of their race.

In June 1956, the US Supreme Court declared racial segregation on buses unconstitutional and people of any color were allowed to sit wherever they wanted. Rosa became known as the "mother of the civil rights movement." The civil rights movement was an important organization which fought to end racial discrimination.

STAND UP TO RACISM

Imagine that you are on vacation in a country where everyone believes that people have certain characteristics just because of the way they look.

Look at the table below and tick the statements that apply to you.

My hair is ... *(check the box that applies to you)*		This means ...
Red	☐	you can run really fast
Brown	☐	you can sing beautifully
Black	☐	you are brilliant at math
Blonde	☐	you can play the piano
Other hair color	☐	you are an incredible dancer

My eyes are ... *(check the box that applies to you)*		This means ...
Green	☐	you are forgetful
Brown	☐	you are clumsy
Blue or gray	☐	you are lazy
Hazel	☐	you are rude

What assumptions would the people of this country make about you? Can you think of how they might treat you differently based on these assumptions? Is that fair?

- -

- -

- -

- -

THE BUS ON WHICH ROSA REFUSED
TO GIVE UP HER SEAT

ROSALIND FRANKLIN

BRITISH SCIENTIST

1920 - 1958

AGE 6

Rosalind spends her free time doing math calculations.

Age 15

She selects Arthur Eddington's book *New Pathways in Science* (topics include subatomic energy and quantum theory) as her prize for winning a school competition.

AGE 21

Rosalind graduates with second-class honors. Even though she's super-bright, she's a perfectionist and spends too long composing perfect answers to the first questions in the exams, and doesn't leave enough time to finish.

Age 18

She arrives at Cambridge University to study natural sciences. She makes a complaint about the standard of the chemistry lectures and the lectures improve.

Age 31

Rosalind uses X-rays to take photos of DNA. This leads to the discovery of DNA's double-helix structure. Her discovery is one of the turning points in the history of science.

AGE 22

She makes discoveries about the properties of coal that play an important part in fueling Britain's effort in the war against Nazi Germany.

AGE 37

Rosalind dies before she can be awarded a Nobel Prize for her work. Instead, this goes to James Watson and Francis Crick, who used her research to advance their theories.

Celebrate YOUR DIFFERENCES

Unless you have an identical twin, no one has exactly the same DNA as you. It's responsible for making you look the way you look—it gives your hair, eyes, and skin their natural color. But actually, about 99.9% of the DNA of every person on the planet is identical. It's only that 0.1% that makes you unique.

DRAW A PICTURE OF YOURSELF AND ONE OF YOUR FRIENDS IN THE BOXES BELOW.

Me

My friend

IN WHAT WAYS ARE YOU THE SAME? IN WHAT WAYS ARE YOU DIFFERENT?

- -

- -

- -

- -

WHAT IS DNA?

DNA stands for deoxyribonucleic acid. It's a code in genes that determines all the characteristics of a living thing. As Rosalind discovered, DNA is in the shape of a double helix, and looks a bit like a twisted ladder.

Sarah
EMMA EDMONDS

Canadian soldier and spy

1841 - 1898

PIRATES AND ADVENTURING

As a child Sarah worked on her parents' farm, riding horses and shooting game with great skill. Her heroine was Fanny Campbell, the female pirate captain of Maturin Murray Ballou's book of the same name. Fanny dressed as a man to go adventuring, which put an idea into Sarah's head.

WHO WAS FRANKLIN FLINT THOMPSON?

When Sarah's father tried to force her into marriage, Sarah ran away from home and crossed the border into America. To avoid being found, she disguised herself as a man named Franklin Thompson and enlisted in the army to fight in the American Civil War. She was a fearless soldier and a master of disguise. She was even sent on intelligence missions across enemy lines "disguised" as a woman!

DANGER OF DISCOVERY

When Sarah contracted malaria, she worried that her real identity would be discovered, so she left the army and went to a private hospital. "Franklin Thompson" had disappeared and was accused of being a deserter, and Sarah would have been executed if she'd gone back to being him after she recovered. Instead, she decided to serve as a female nurse.

HOORAY FOR SARAH!

Sarah published her story in a book and when her comrades learned of her true identity they appealed to the government to drop the charge of desertion. Later, Sarah was given the military honors she deserved.

For the love of your country

It was patriotism, or love of her country, that inspired Sarah's success. And even though Sarah was born in Canada, she felt deeply patriotic toward America. How do you feel about the country that you live in?

Write down five things that you like about where you live:

1. _____
2. _____
3. _____
4. _____
5. _____

If you could live anywhere in the world, where would it be?

_____

_____

_____

IS THERE ANOTHER COUNTRY THAT YOU ADMIRE? WHAT DO YOU LIKE ABOUT IT?

_____

_____

_____

_____

_____

_____

_____

Sarah disguised as Franklin Thompson

SIMONE de Beauvoir

1908 - 1986

French philosopher

Simone was born into a wealthy family. After World War I the family lost much of their money and could no longer afford to employ cleaners. Simone saw that it was her mother and not her father who started doing all the jobs in the home, and she thought that this was really unfair. Simone's mother didn't like doing all the housework, but she felt that she had to because she was a woman.

Simone believed that women should be free to do what they liked and not what society expected of them. She published her ideas in a book called *The Second Sex*. Many people agreed with her and she became known as "the mother of feminism."

Simone believed that education could help women to become free. She studied mathematics, languages, and literature, and then went on to complete a degree in philosophy. At college she met a student called Jean-Paul Sartre, and together they developed ideas about a field of philosophy called "existentialism." Simone published many books and articles about ways of thinking and living.

I DO, DO YOU?

Jean-Paul asked Simone to marry him, but Simone said "no" even though she loved him. She wanted to be free! The pair never married, never had children, and never lived together, and yet remained close until they died.

WHAT IS *existentialism?*

EXISTENTIALISM IS A PHILOSOPHY THAT FOCUSES ON A PERSON'S FREEDOM AND CHOICE. IT SUPPORTS THE VIEW THAT HUMAN BEINGS DEFINE THEIR OWN MEANING IN LIFE AND DETERMINE THEIR OWN PATH THROUGH DELIBERATE DECISIONS.

WOMEN ARE MADE,

not born

Do you think there are still times when girls are expected to behave in a certain way just because they're female? One way of checking society's attitudes toward gender roles is to look at advertising. Flick through a magazine or toy catalog, or watch some TV ads, and fill in the chart to show each time you see a male or a female doing each of the activities.

	MALE	FEMALE
Shown indoors		
Shown outdoors		
Being loud		
Being quiet		
Playing sports		
Being creative		
Doing housework		
Doing paid work		
Taking care of someone		
Fixing or building something		

Look at the chart you have filled in. What are women most likely to be shown doing as opposed to men? What do you think about this?

Simone Veil

1927 - 2017

Simone's parents had three daughters and a son and they enjoyed a happy life. As Simone entered her teenage years World War II broke out. Two days after Simone completed some important exams, her entire family was arrested because they were Jewish. They were sent to concentration camps and only the three daughters survived.

In 1974 Simone became France's Minister of Health and worked to end various forms of discrimination against women. She dramatically improved the rights of women in family legal matters and in health and maternity care.

The horrific events of Simone's early life led her to believe that the key to peace was a united and cooperative Europe. She embarked on a political career, first gaining a diploma in law and political science, and then passing the very difficult exams to become a magistrate. She specialized in the rights of women and prisoners.

In 1979 Simone became the first elected President of the European Parliament. She was a champion of peace and always acted with conviction. When she died in 2017 it was announced that she would be buried in the Panthéon, a mausoleum reserved for the most adored cultural and historical figures in France's history.

get DEBATING!

Simone was a powerful speaker and argued passionately in debates at the highest level. A debate is a formal presentation of the arguments for and against an issue. Try writing some arguments for and against the statements below.

Parents should be allowed to choose their baby's gender.

FOR

AGAINST

Learning about the past is important.

FOR

AGAINST

Video games are too violent.

FOR

AGAINST

Homework should be banned.

FOR

AGAINST

Sojourner TRUTH

AFRICAN-AMERICAN ABOLITIONIST

1797 - 1883

SOJOURNER TRUTH WAS BORN INTO SLAVERY. HER NAME WAS ISABELLA BAUMFREE. SHE AND HER SIBLINGS WERE SLAVES WHO COULD BE BOUGHT AND SOLD AT ANY TIME. ONE DAY SHE WOULD BE PLAYING WITH ONE OF HER SISTERS, AND THE NEXT DAY THAT SISTER WOULD BE GONE.

AGE 9
SOLD AT AUCTION ALONG WITH A FLOCK OF SHEEP FOR $100

AGE 11
SOLD FOR $105

AGE 13
SOLD FOR $175

Life was very hard for Sojourner. She married and had five children, and her greatest fear was that her children would be sold and that she'd never get to see them again. When Sojourner was 28 she was told that because her work was so good she would be freed the following year. But then when the time came her owner changed his mind. Sojourner was furious and escaped with her infant daughter, but had to leave her other children behind. She met a couple who agreed to buy her and then free her.

AGE 29
SOLD FOR $20 AND THEN **FREED!**

Then Sojourner's worst nightmare came true: her 5-year-old son had been sold illegally. Sojourner decided to take the guilty man to court. It was a brave move for a female slave to do this, but she won the case! This gave lots of other people hope. Sojourner began to travel the country, fired up by her religious zeal, telling her story, speaking out against slavery, and fighting for women's rights.

The campaign to abolish
SLAVERY

abolition of SLAVERY

When the campaign to abolish slavery began, around 250 years ago, there were no TV bulletins or Internet stories to tell the people about the terrible conditions in which slaves were living. One solution was to grab people's attention with an eye-catching poster. Design your own slavery abolition poster with the intention of making people in the street stop and think.

Sophie Scholl

GERMAN POLITICAL ACTIVIST

1921 - 1943

Sophie had a happy, carefree childhood. When Adolf Hitler rose to power Sophie joined a group associated with his Nazi Party called the League of German Girls. It wasn't long, however, before she started to question the party's beliefs and behavior. In 1935 the Nazis passed the Nuremberg Laws. These laws restricted the movement and activities of Jewish people and declared them non-citizens. Sophie complained when two of her Jewish friends were prevented from joining her group.

Sophie began to hear about the terrible things the Nazi party were doing, but expressing criticism was very dangerous. Sophie's father was jailed for making a negative comment to one of his colleagues about Hitler, and Sophie's brothers were arrested for their involvement in a free-thinking group that was part of the German Youth Movement.

Sophie decided that she couldn't stand back and let the Nazis continue, even if it meant risking her life. She and some friends formed a group called the White Rose. Together they wrote six anti-Nazi resistance leaflets and distributed them across Munich.

In 1943 Sophie and other members of the White Rose were arrested for their activities, and after a short trial were sentenced to death. Sophie was calm and courageous as she went to meet her executioner. She believed that her death was unimportant, unless it stirred others to action.

CIVIL Courage

Civil courage involves standing up in public against something you believe is wrong, even if you run the risk of being punished or harmed. What are the characteristics of someone who shows strong civil courage? Write one word in each of the rose's petals.

Can you think of a time when you've shown civil courage?

MAYBE YOU'VE STOOD UP TO A BULLY, OR TOLD SOMEONE OFF FOR DROPPING LITTER. HOW DID IT MAKE YOU FEEL?

What HAPPENED to Turia?

When Turia was 24 she was working as a mining engineer and spent her free time training as an athlete. While racing in a 100-kilometer ultramarathon in the Australian outback she became trapped in a grass fire. She received severe burns to 65% of her body and lost seven fingers.

Turia PITT

Australian humanitarian and motivator

BORN 1987

How did SHE COPE?

Turia's appearance was completely transformed and her injuries meant she'd lost much of her independence. For many people, life as they knew it would have been over, but not for Turia. She took what could have been a tragedy and turned it into something shining with positivity.

WHAT DID SHE ACHIEVE?

After two years in recovery and over 200 operations, she started competing in ironman competitions, proving that, with the right mindset, there's nothing you can't achieve. Turia became an ambassador for Interplast, a charity that provides life-changing reconstructive surgery to people in developing countries. The huge sums of money she raised made a difference to thousands of people's lives.

Make POSITIVITY PETALS

Turia believes that life is 10% what happens to us and 90% how we respond. Make a positive-thinking flower to keep in your pocket. When times get tough, open a petal and remind yourself to think like Turia!

1.

DRAW OR TRACE A HEXAGON WITH PETALS LIKE THE ONE BELOW ON TO A PIECE OF CARD. CUT OUT YOUR FLOWER.

I can do this

I believe in myself

I am strong

My POSITIVE-THINKING flower

I am enough

Today I am a leader

Today will be an awesome day

2.

WRITE A POSITIVE STATEMENT ON EACH OF THE PETALS.

3.

FOLD THE PETALS INTO THE CENTER. KEEP YOUR FLOWER IN YOUR POCKET OR PENCIL CASE AND BRING IT OUT WHENEVER YOU NEED IT.

Venus and Serena WILLIAMS

VENUS, BORN 1980

SERENA, BORN 1981

AMERICAN TENNIS PLAYERS

These sibling tennis players are two of the most successful athletes in the world. They have even played against each other in nine Grand Slam singles finals and both have been ranked by the Women's Tennis Association at the World No.1 position. Talk about sibling rivalry.

Their dad began teaching them tennis when they were little more than toddlers, and he moved the family from California to Florida when the budding tennis stars were 10 and 11 years old, to enroll them in Rick Macci's Delray Beach Tennis Academy. They trained six hours a day, six days a week. Their dedication paid off and each landed a $12-million sponsorship deal in their early teens.

Competitiveness has brought the sisters very close. Venus and Serena support each other even when they're playing in the same tournaments. They even play doubles tennis together and have won 22 titles including 14 Grand Slams and 3 Olympic gold medals.

Wins to date ... and counting!

	VENUS	SERENA
Women's singles titles	49	72
Women's doubles titles	22	23
Grand Slam women's singles titles	7	23
Grand Slam women's doubles titles	14	14
Grand Slam mixed doubles titles	2	2

TRAIN LIKE A TENNIS PRO

Tennis players need excellent hand-eye coordination. Develop yours by practicing these skills. With a ball, see how many times you can do each of the challenges below in 1 minute. Don't worry if you drop the ball, just pick it up and carry on. Keep practicing and try to beat your personal best!

THROW THE BALL IN THE AIR AND CATCH IT IN BOTH HANDS.

Attempt 1:   Attempt 2:   Attempt 3:

THROW THE BALL FROM ONE HAND TO THE OTHER.

Attempt 1:   Attempt 2:   Attempt 3:

THROW THE BALL AGAINST A WALL AND CATCH IT BEFORE IT HITS THE GROUND

Attempt 1:   Attempt 2:   Attempt 3:

STAND IN YOUR BEDROOM DOORWAY AND THROW THE BALL SO IT LANDS ON YOUR PILLOW.

Attempt 1:   Attempt 2:   Attempt 3:

Wangari MAATHAI

"Until you dig a hole, you plant a tree, you water it and make it survive, you haven't done a thing. You are just talking."

1940 – 2011

KENYAN ACTIVIST

When Wangari was growing up in Kenya in the 1940s she was surrounded by thick forests, clean water, rich soils, and plenty of food. The land was beautiful and she was happy. She worked hard at school and won a scholarship to study in the USA. Later she became the first woman in East and Central Africa to obtain a PhD.

After teaching at the University of Nairobi, Wangari returned to her home. The lives of the people living there had become very difficult. The government had allowed the forests to be cut down to make way for plantations. The soil was eroding and the women had to walk long distances to find firewood and clean water. No one had enough to eat.

Why not plant trees? thought Wangari. So she did. She founded the Green Belt Movement and taught women about the connection between the environment and their quality of life. Together, Wangari and the women planted more than 35 million trees. They worked against deforestation, poverty, and inequality. Like the trees, the Green Belt Movement grew strong and powerful. The government tried to silence Wangari, but she could not be stopped. She became the first African woman to win the Nobel Peace Prize for her work.

TAKING ROOT

WANGARI THOUGHT THAT EVERYONE SHOULD PLANT A TREE. WHY NOT PLANT SOME SEEDS OF YOUR OWN? HERE'S HOW ...

YOU WILL NEED:

* A small plant pot
* Permanent marker pen
* Soil
* Something to scoop soil
* Seeds

1. Write the name of what plant your seeds will grow on the side of your pot.

2. Scoop some soil into the pot until it almost reaches the top.

3. TAKE A FEW SEEDS AND GENTLY PUSH THEM INTO THE SOIL, COVERING THEM WITH A LITTLE OF THE SOIL AFTERWARD.

4. Put your plant pot in a sunny spot and sprinkle with a little water every day.

XIAN Zhang

CHINESE CONDUCTOR

BORN 1973

Age 3

Xian's mother gives Xian her first piano lessons. Pianos were banned during the Cultural Revolution in China, which had just finished. Xian's dad found an old broken piano and repaired it for his daughter.

Age 8

Xian's parents decide she needs proper piano lessons and they make a 12-hour round trip each week to the conservatoire in Shenyang.

Age 20

Xian steps in for her teacher and conducts *The Marriage of Figaro* for the China National Opera Orchestra. She does a brilliant job.

Age 13

She wins a place to study musicology, conducting and composing at the Beijing conservatoire.

Age 36

Xian lands a job leading the Orchestra Sinfonica di Milano Giuseppe Verdi and becomes the first woman to be named Music Director of an Italian symphony orchestra.

Age 28

She enters her first conductor competition and wins! She is whisked off to New York to assist the famous conductor Lorin Maazel at the New York Philharmonic.

Age 42

Xian becomes the first female conductor to be named Music Director of the New Jersey Symphony Orchestra. She also joins the BBC National Orchestra of Wales as Principal Guest Conductor.

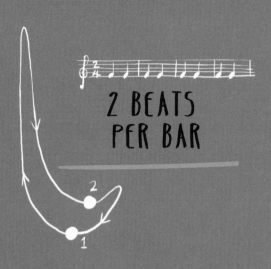

2 BEATS PER BAR

3 BEATS PER BAR

COULD YOU BE A
conductor?

Conductors lead and direct orchestras or musical groups using either their hands or a baton. They use their skill and knowledge to bring the music to life, and to make sure that all the musicians play at the same speed and at the same time. Want to give it a go?

Grab a pencil or something similar to use as a baton, choose a time signature below, then move the pencil through the air in the pattern shown.

4 BEATS PER BAR

WHAT IS A TIME SIGNATURE?

Time signatures are used in music to write down how many beats there are in a measure, or "bar."

ZAHA
Hadid
IRAQI ARCHITECT

1950 - 2016

If you were to draw a quick sketch of a building, chances are it would have straight sides and is either a square or a rectangle, right? When Zaha Hadid imagined buildings they didn't look like that at all. In fact, they looked more like this ...

Heydar Aliyev Center, Azerbaijan,
FOR WHICH ZAHA WON THE LONDON DESIGN MUSEUM'S DESIGN OF THE YEAR AWARD.

As a child Zaha loved maths and art, so when she grew up she became an architect. The fluid, gravity-defying buildings she'd spent her whole life imagining were made in the real world.

It took a while for people to believe in her designs but when they did she created the most incredible buildings: the Vitra Fire Station in Germany; the MAXXI Museum of 21st Century Art in Rome; the London Aquatics Centre. She won all kinds of prestigious awards, including the Pritzker Prize, and was the first woman to win the Royal Institute of British Architects Gold Medal.

Zaha wanted to create buildings that flowed through space, and that would shape how people move through that space. She had a powerful imagination, a powerful personality, and a huge amount of skill. She became known as the "queen of the curve."

WHO NEEDS GRAVITY?

MANY OF ZAHA'S DESIGNS LOOK LIKE THEY WOULD BE IMPOSSIBLE TO BUILD IN REAL LIFE, BUT SHE WASN'T THE KIND OF PERSON WHO WOULD LET SOMETHING LIKE THE LAWS OF PHYSICS STAND IN HER WAY. NOW IT'S YOUR TURN TO FOLLOW IN HER FOOTSTEPS. IMAGINE YOU'RE AN ARCHITECT AND YOU'VE BEEN ASKED TO DESIGN A NEW LIBRARY THAT WILL INSPIRE A LOVE OF BOOKS. LET YOUR IMAGINATION RUN WILD!

I AM A wonder woman

. . . .

(YOUR NAME)

. . . .

(YOUR DATE OF BIRTH)

The story so far

Tell the story of your life so far—you can use a timeline
of dates/your ages or make it more of a story.

MY PROUDEST MOMENTS

Think of 3 moments from your life that fill you with happiness and pride.

What's next?

THE WOMEN IN THIS BOOK HAD BIG DREAMS AND WORKED HARD TO MAKE THEM COME TRUE. WHAT ARE YOUR OWN DREAMS FOR ...

... the next year?

... the next 10 years?

... for your lifetime?

Index